T0328678

Cambridge Elements ≡

Elements in Bioethics and Neuroethics
edited by
Thomasine Kushner
California Pacific Medical Center, San Francisco

RESPONSIBILITY FOR HEALTH

Sven Ove Hansson
*Karolinska Institutet and
KTH Royal Institute of Technology*

CAMBRIDGE
UNIVERSITY PRESS

CAMBRIDGE
UNIVERSITY PRESS

University Printing House, Cambridge CB2 8BS, United Kingdom

One Liberty Plaza, 20th Floor, New York, NY 10006, USA

477 Williamstown Road, Port Melbourne, VIC 3207, Australia

314–321, 3rd Floor, Plot 3, Splendor Forum, Jasola District Centre,
New Delhi – 110025, India

103 Penang Road, #05–06/07, Visioncrest Commercial, Singapore 238467

Cambridge University Press is part of the University of Cambridge.

It furthers the University's mission by disseminating knowledge in the pursuit of education, learning, and research at the highest international levels of excellence.

www.cambridge.org
Information on this title: www.cambridge.org/9781009247276
DOI: 10.1017/9781009247290

First published 2022

A catalogue record for this publication is available from the British Library.

ISBN 978-1-009-24727-6 Paperback
ISSN 2752-3934 (online)
ISSN 2752-3926 (print)

Cambridge University Press has no responsibility for the persistence or accuracy of URLs for external or third-party internet websites referred to in this publication and does not guarantee that any content on such websites is, or will remain, accurate or appropriate.

Every effort has been made in preparing this Element to provide accurate and up-to-date information which is in accord with accepted standards and practice at the time of publication. Although case histories are drawn from actual cases, every effort has been made to disguise the identities of the individuals involved. Nevertheless, the authors, editors and publishers can make no warranties that the information contained herein is totally free from error, not least because clinical standards are constantly changing through research and regulation. The authors, editors and publishers therefore disclaim all liability for direct or consequential damages resulting from the use of material contained in this Element. Readers are strongly advised to pay careful attention to information provided by the manufacturer of any drugs or equipment that they plan to use.

Responsibility for Health

Elements in Bioethics and Neuroethics

DOI: 10.1017/9781009247290
First published online: July 2022

Sven Ove Hansson
Karolinska Institutet and KTH Royal Institute of Technology
Author for correspondence: Sven Ove Hansson, soh@kth.se

Abstract: This Element offers a broad perspective on responsibility for health. This includes responsibilities in the prevention of disease and accidents and in the creation of health care for all. The professional responsibilities of physicians and nurses are explored, and so are the responsibilities that we all have for our own health. Many of the central problems in health care ethics are discussed in a responsibility perspective – for instance, paternalism, informed consent, evidence-based medicine, alternative medicine, and the use of artificial intelligence in health care. In order to perform this analysis, conceptual tools for responsibility analysis are provided, such as the distinction between blame responsibility and task responsibility and various notions of causality that are relevant for our understanding of responsibility.

Keywords: Responsibility, public health, universal health care, justice, social contagion, globalization

ISBNs: 9781009247276 (PB), 9781009247290 (OC)
ISSNs: 2752-3934 (online), 2752-3926 (print)

Contents

1 Introduction

Most of the discussion on responsibility and health has focused on each person's responsibility for her own health. Here we will take a much broader perspective. We will investigate responsibilities in the prevention of disease and accidents, in the creation of health care for all, and in the professional delivery of health care. Many of the central problems in health care ethics will be discussed from a responsibility perspective – for instance, paternalism, informed consent, evidence-based medicine, alternative medicine, and the use of artificial intelligence in health care.

To begin with, we need to sharpen our conceptual tools. Section 2 introduces the distinction between blame and task responsibility, and explains why these two forms of responsibility should not always coincide. This section also clarifies the relation between responsibility and causality and shows why we need a multifactorial concept of causality.

Section 3 provides another necessary background, namely on the causation of diseases. After an examination of the nature–nurture issue, some major preventable factors underlying the global burden of disease are briefly introduced. A causal analysis of the obesity epidemic is used to exemplify the differences between an individual and a public health perspective on a disease.

Section 4 begins by showing how much our health-related habits depend on our social environment. This is followed by an ethical discussion of our responsibilities for each other's health. Each of us can contribute in many small ways to the prevention of diseases and accidents. In arguing that we also have a responsibility to do so, I appeal to traditional moral principles such as the virtues of setting good examples and doing one's part in joint endeavors. The section concludes with a discussion of possible conflicts between liberty and public health measures.

Section 5 is devoted to the aim of health care for all. It has a particular emphasis on the possibilities and challenges for low- and middle-income countries striving to achieve that goal. Positive experiences from several countries show that it is indeed achievable and that the costs are not insurmountable.

Section 6 discusses the responsibilities of professional health care providers. The main focus is on the responsibility to offer patients the best available treatment and on the knowledge base for fulfilling that responsibility. The section ends with a discussion of the impact that the use of artificial intelligence can have on professional responsibilities in health care.

Section 7 turns to the responsibility that we all have for our own health. It begins by describing and endorsing an approach to patient responsibility in health care that strives to empower patients and avoid putting blame on them.

This is followed by a critical discussion of proposals that go in the very opposite direction, putting more blame on patients and even denying them treatment if they are deemed to have caused their own disease.

Finally, Section 8 summarizes some of the main conclusions in the form of four guidelines that cover both disease prevention and health care.

2 What Is Responsibility?

The words "responsible" and "responsibility" derive from the Latin verb "respondere," which means to answer or respond. The English verb "answer" derives from an old Germanic word ("andsuarian" in Old English), which originally meant to answer for or be responsible for something. In some other Germanic languages, the word has retained that meaning; for instance, in both Danish and Swedish, "ansvar" means responsibility. The etymology reveals a close connection between being responsible and having to answer for something.

2.1 Two Ways to Be Responsible

In today's language, the term "responsibility" is employed in many ways and in many contexts, but for practical purposes, it is usually sufficient to distinguish between two main meanings. One of these is *blame responsibility*. This is the type of responsibility that a person has if she is considered culpable or blame-worthy when something goes wrong. For instance, suppose that in order not to miss a cinema show, you rush down the stairs so fast that you lose control and run into a fragile old person who is severely hurt in the fall. You will then be held responsible in the sense that you can legitimately be blamed and criticized for what happened.[1]

The other major type is *task responsibility*. It means that you are required to make sure that something happens. Suppose that as a member of the local film society, you have undertaken to rent the films for the next three meetings. Then you have to make sure that the films are rented and properly delivered. This does not necessarily mean that you have to do the work yourself. You can fulfill your task responsibility by making sure that someone else fulfills it.

The terms "blame responsibility" and "task responsibility" were proposed by the American philosopher Robert Goodin.[2] Unfortunately, there is considerable terminological confusion in this area. In his pioneering work on responsibility, H. L. A. Hart used the term "role-responsibility" for the "specific duties" that a person obtains by occupying "a distinctive place or office in a social organization."[3] He used the word "role" in a wide sense, and others who use the term have further extended it.[4] Thus, in common usage, role responsibility includes not only the roles we have as professionals, employees, or functionaries in an organization, but also private roles such as that of a spouse or parent, as well as temporary roles that originate in agreements such as to water someone's flowers or feed a pet lizard. The major reason for preferring the term "task responsibility" to "role responsibility" is that it conveys this wide usage more clearly.

Hart's term for what we now call "blame responsibility" was "liability-responsibility." This term was suitable since his primary focus lay on legal responsibilities. After giving an account of legal liability-responsibility, he discussed how the concept could be applied in a moral context, and proposed that the phrases "deserving blame," "blameworthy," and "morally bound to make amends or pay compensation" would be appropriate.[5] From this, it is no big step to replace the term "liability" with "blame" in discussions of moral responsibility.

It has become common to use temporal terms to distinguish between blame and task responsibility. Blame responsibility is called "backward-looking responsibility," "retrospective responsibility," or "historic responsibility." Similarly, task responsibility is called "forward-looking responsibility" or "prospective responsibility."[6] Unfortunately, this terminology tends to conflate two crossing distinctions, namely on the one hand the distinction between blame and task responsibility, and on the other hand that between responsibilities concerning the past and the future. All four combinations are important to discuss, as shown in the following examples:

(1) *Blame responsibility for past actions*: Who is to be blamed for the insufficient pandemic preparedness at the outbreak of the COVID-19 pandemic?

(2) *Blame responsibility for future actions*: Who should be held responsible if pandemic preparedness is not improved in the next few years?

(3) *Task responsibility for past actions*: Was the government in the 1950s morally required to make sure that the whole population had access to affordable health care?

(4) *Task responsibility for future actions*: Is the current government morally required to ensure that the best available medical treatments are made freely available to the whole population?

Terms like "backward-looking" for blame responsibility and "forward-looking" for task responsibility tend to put the whole focus on cases (1) and (4). This is unfortunate since the other two cases are also in need of careful analysis.

Before we leave the terminological issue, a problem with the term "blame responsibility" should be mentioned. Already in the article where Goodin introduced it, he recognized that we can appraise people's actions not only negatively but also positively. He intended "blame responsibility" to cover the assignment of "credit or, more commonly, blame for certain sorts of states of affairs."[7] Arguably, we should pay more attention to the positive version of blame responsibility. One option would be to introduce the term "praise responsibility" for it. Another more drastic change would be to introduce a neutral term such as "appraisal responsibility" to cover both blame responsibility and its positive variant. However, in order to avoid adding to the oversupply of terms in this area, no terminological reform will be attempted here. The established terms "blame responsibility" and "task responsibility" will be used for the two main forms of responsibility.

2.2 Disconnections between Blame and Task Responsibility

Blame and task responsibility often come together. One important mechanism that connects them is our tendency to assign blame responsibility to people who fail to fulfill a task responsibility. Suppose that you have paid me a small sum of money to mow your lawn once a week when you are on vacation. If you come home and find meter-high grass in your backyard, then you will probably put blame responsibility on me for neglecting my task responsibility.

There is also another major mechanism that brings blame and task responsibility together: after a wrongdoing, we often assign both types of responsibility to the wrongdoer – a blame responsibility for the wrong that was done and a task responsibility to do better in the future. Suppose that Susan drives drunk and runs into a parked car, damaging it severely. We will then hold her blame responsible, in the sense that she is to be blamed for what happened and should compensate the owner of the wrecked vehicle. At the same time, this episode accentuates her task responsibility to make sure that she never drives drunk in the future.

However, these connections do not always hold. In many situations, blame and task responsibility come apart. One common reason for this is that we tend to excuse a person who has failed in her task responsibilities if she did her very best but the task was too difficult for her. Then the failed task responsibility is not followed by blame responsibility.[8] Another reason is that we sometimes prefer to assign task responsibilities to people, not because they can be blamed for a problem but rather because they are in the best position to solve it. Such efficiency-based assignments of task responsibilities were instrumental in the development of modern safety management.

Throughout the nineteenth century, industrial workplace accidents were largely blamed on workers, who were assigned both blame responsibility for the accidents that occurred and task responsibility for avoiding accidents by working carefully. In the early twentieth century, this approach was successfully challenged by both workers and accident researchers. The American sociologist Crystal Eastman (1881–1928) performed detailed studies of a large number of accidents. She found that the same types of accidents took place again and again. Her detailed analysis of the accidents also showed that they could have been prevented by technical measures such as protective fencing, emergency stops, and so forth. To prevent workplace accidents, it was much more efficient to improve equipment and routines than to admonish workers to be careful. Consequently, task responsibilities had to be assigned to the employer, who had the powers necessary to introduce new equipment and routines.[9] Making employers (task) responsible for workplace safety turned out to be highly successful. During the twentieth century, the frequency of workplace fatalities and injuries declined drastically in most industrialized countries, although there is still much room for improvement.

In the late twentieth and early twenty-first century, we have seen a similar development in traffic safety. After many decades of propaganda for careful driving, it has become more and more clear that only relatively little can be achieved in that way. Traffic safety specialists now start out from the insight that humans inevitably make mistakes. Consequently, traffic systems have to be reconstructed so that human mistakes do not lead to fatalities and severe injuries. Just as technical solutions should prevent injuries if a worker operating a machine puts her hand in the wrong place, the traffic system should prevent injuries if a driver makes a mistake. To achieve this, major task responsibilities have to be assigned to car manufacturers and to the designers and managers of roads.[10]

The assignment of task responsibilities to employers for workplace safety and to car manufacturers and road managers for traffic safety does not necessarily involve any assignment of blame responsibility. They receive this task responsibility because they have unique powers and abilities to reduce the number of accidents. This is a ground for task responsibilities that we will return to in the coming sections.

2.3 Similarities between the Two Types of Responsibility

Although they do not always coincide, blame and task responsibility have many features in common, three of which are particularly important for studies of responsibility and health.

First, both blame and task responsibility can be either legal or moral. A person who has damaged someone else's property can be morally blamed for this, and her moral blame responsibility typically includes paying an appropriate compensation. At the same time, she can be legally blame responsible (or liability-responsible in Hart's terminology). Then she can be legally forced to pay compensation and perhaps also legally punished for causing the damage. The law also assigns quite a few task responsibilities. A parent is legally task responsible for the child's welfare, an external auditor for the accuracy of the audit report, and a judge for ensuring lawful procedures and correct interpretations of the law.

The second common feature is that both blame and task responsibilities can be shared, in the sense that several persons can have one and the same responsibility. However, the sharing of responsibilities is not a zero-sum game. In other words, it is not like sharing a cake. The more people you divide a cake between, the smaller share will each of them have. This is not how sharing of responsibilities works.[11] In many cases, responsibility is more similar to the fairy-tale cake that grows each time you share it, so that everyone gets a piece of the same size as the original cake.

Parenthood is a good example of how this works for task responsibilities. If a child has two parents, then each of them has the same responsibility for the child's welfare that a single parent would have had. Each parent has the full responsibility and has to step in if the other parent fails. Another example is responsibility for avoiding traffic accidents. Suppose that the government substantially steps up its traffic safety activities and starts to take responsibility for safe roads in a way that it did not do before. This does not reduce the responsibility of individual road users. Their responsibility for driving safely is the same, and neither speeding nor drunk driving has become more morally acceptable.

Shared blame responsibilities are perhaps best illustrated by cases of so-called over-determination.[12] Suppose that Anastasia has a severe nut allergy. Both Cyril and David tell her that the cake on the table is nut free. Unfortunately, they are wrong, and she has a severe anaphylaxis. It would seem unreasonable for either Cyril or David to try to reduce their blame responsibility by pointing at the other's mistake. Each of them has the same blame responsibility as if he had been the only person who said anything to her about the cake. To sum up, neither blame nor task responsibility is necessarily diminished when it is shared.

The third common feature of blame and task responsibility is that you are usually not only (blame or task) responsible *for* something but also *to* someone. If you are blame responsible for some undesired event, then you are blame responsible to those who are negatively affected by that event. If you are task responsible, then there are usually people who can legitimately demand that you fulfill the task, and it is to them that you are task responsible.

In some cases, responsibility is *to* and *for* the same person. The responsibility of parents is a prime example. As a parent you are (task) responsible for many aspects of your child's life. Ultimately this is also a responsibility *to* your child, since it is the child that has the right to your efforts and devotion. Another example is a physician's (task) responsibility for offering a patient the best available treatment. This is primarily a responsibility to the patient.

A person can also be blame or task responsible to herself. Someone who bought a bunch of expensive clothes a week before payday and now has no money to buy food might be told, "You only have yourself to blame." This is another way of saying that she carries the whole blame responsibility for her predicament. A spoiled youth who has recently moved out of his parents' house but still tries to engage them in all kinds of daily chores can be told that "this is now your own responsibility." This implies that he has a task responsibility to himself, namely a responsibility for his own housework. The possibility of a responsibility to oneself is important in a health care context. It means that we cannot for *conceptual* reasons exclude that someone is (blame or task) responsible for their own health.

2.4 What Is Causality?

Blame and task responsibility also have something more fundamental in common: they are both closely connected to causality. With few exceptions, we only hold people blame responsible for events that they caused or at least contributed to causally.[13] Similarly, we normally only assign task responsibility to persons deemed to have the abilities or "causal powers" to fulfill the task.

One might hope that causality should provide a secure and objective ground for our deliberations on responsibility. But unfortunately, our common conceptions of causality are much less robust than what we tend to believe. To begin with, it is necessary to distinguish between two senses of causality. First, there is a general notion of causality that refers to how the world hangs together. This includes all the interdependencies that obtain among objects and events in the world, all the ways in which what happens in some points in space-time restricts or determines what happens at other points in space-time. We can call this *world causality*. It is a feature of the world we are living in.

The other notion of causality is the pattern of cause-effect relationships that we refer to when describing how events hang together. Such relationships are highly useful for describing and understanding much of what we can observe. Someone throws a brick at a window, and the window breaks. We describe this as a connection between the throw, which is the cause, and the shattering of the pane, which is the effect. This is an example of *CE causality*, the ascription of a cause to an event which is then called an effect of that cause.

Based on such simple examples, we often equate world causality with CE causality, but in general, world causality is much too complex to be captured by CE causality.[14] One of the best examples of this is the pattern of movements in the Solar System of planets, moons, comets, and other astronomical objects. We cannot adequately explain their patterns of movement with CE causality, since this would limit us to connections in which one movement gives rise to another. That is not how the universe works. Instead, the movements in the Solar System have to be understood as the combined outcome of a large number of simultaneous mutual influences. The same applies to most other complex systems studied by scientists, including ecosystems, economic and social systems, and not least the human body.[15]

Whereas world causality is a feature of the world, CE causality is a model we use to describe and understand the world. It is no doubt a highly successful model. We use it incessantly, both in everyday life and in a wide range of scientific endeavors. Medical knowledge about disease processes and treatment effects can often be usefully summarized as cause-effect relationships. However, it is important to keep in mind that nevertheless, CE causality is a model. Like all other models, it represents reality less than perfectly.

2.5 The Multiplicity of Causal Factors

In the health context, the major problem with the CE model is that it does not account for the multiplicity of causal factors that influence our bodies. Instead of a single cause, there are in most cases several causal factors that contribute in different ways to an effect. The question of what causes cholera is a classic example of this. A bacteriologist would typically tell you that this disease is caused by the cholera bacterium, *Vibrio cholera*. However, if you ask an epidemiologist what causes the disease, you will probably be told that it is caused by inadequate sanitation.[16] There is no contradiction between these two answers. They just put focus on different parts of the process that leads to the disease. However, the example shows that the common practice of assigning a single cause to an effect can restrict our understanding. If you only know one of the two answers, then you have an incomplete understanding of what causes this disease.

Already in the mid-nineteenth century, John Stuart Mill showed that a multiplicity of causal factors is in fact the rule rather than an exception.[17] There is usually more than one causal factor that contributes to an effect. Often it would be appropriate to include them all in our discussions, but as he noted, we have a strong tendency to select one of them and refer to it as "the cause." This choice is not determined by objective factors but rather by our chosen perspective. What we call "the cause" tends to be something we consider to be deviant or conspicuous.[18]

To illustrate this, we can revisit the example of the window pane that broke when a brick was thrown at it. Two obvious causal factors were involved in this event: (1) a brick was thrown at the window, and (2) the window was constructed of a material that breaks when hit by a heavy object, such as a brick. Since we consider the second of these factors to be a normal property of a window pane, we chose the first as "the cause." But let us modify the example. Suppose that the window was made of bulletproof glass, constructed to withstand a much stronger impact than that of a brick thrown at it. In this case, engineers working with ballistic glass would not be satisfied with the causal claim that the breaking of the window was caused by the brick. Instead, they might very well come up with the conclusion that "the cause of the breakage was that the wrong type of polyurethane was used in the manufacturing process."

Unsurprisingly, different social interests can be served by different assignments of causality. This can give rise to a "politics of causality," that is, attempts by different actors to influence public perceptions of causality. For instance, tobacco companies have an interest in downplaying the importance of their own marketing of addictive products and instead describe smoking as the result of a decision by an adult person (although most smokers became addicted before reaching the age of majority). In contrast, health activists call attention to those causal factors behind smoking that government and industry have the power to eliminate. A causal account that puts emphasis on the actions of tobacco companies will support the assignment of far-reaching blame and task responsibilities to these companies. A causal account that emphasizes the actions of individual smokers has the opposite effect.

3 What Determines Our Health?

In order to discuss our responsibilities for health, we need to have a general overview of what determines our health or, as this is also often expressed, the causes of disease and bad health.

3.1 Nature or Nurture?

It was known already in antiquity that some diseases are inherited. For centuries, scientists have disagreed on the relative contributions of on the one hand inborn tendencies ("nature") and on the other hand the influences of the environment and the conditions of life ("nurture"). Today we can express the distinction in a more precise way. We can distinguish between causal factors that are genetic and causal factors in the individual's environment. Genetic and environmental causal factors are by no means mutually exclusive. On the contrary, disease causality typically involves complex interactions among multiple causal factors of both types.

One useful type of investigation that can throw light on the relationship between genetic and environmental factors is studies of identical twins who have for some reason been brought up in different families. This means that they have an identical genetic background but have been subject to different environmental influences. Suppose that in such a study, it turns out that if one member of a separated twin pair has a particular disease, then so almost invariably does the other. This is a strong indication that differences in the environmental conditions to which these twins have been exposed do not have much impact on the incidence of this disease. Conversely, if it is common for only one of the twins in a pair to have the disease, then the variations in living conditions to which these twins were exposed can have had an impact on the disease incidence.

Unfortunately, twin studies are often overinterpreted. If no or only small effects of the environment on a disease can be found in a study, then this is claimed to show that the environmental effects on the disease are small. To see why such a conclusion is unwarranted, let us consider a simple hypothetical example. Suppose that a particular disease manifests itself if and only if two conditions are both satisfied: the individual has a particular gene variant (allele) and she has a high salt intake during childhood. However, this is not known. In order to find out to what extent the disease is genetically determined, a group of researchers perform a twin study. If they perform the study in a country with large variations in salt intake, then there will be quite a few cases in which one member of a twin pair that has the gene will receive a low and the other a high amount of salt in their food. The data from this study will show that the disease has both a genetic and an environmental component. However, if the researchers instead perform the study in a country where everyone eats very salty food, then all twins that have the gene variant associated with the disease will contract the disease. No environmental influences will be found in this study. The general conclusion that we can draw from this example is that important environmental effects on a disease can be missed even in twin studies if the variation of the pertinent environmental factor is too small in the study population.

In the context of public health, environmental factors are often more important to study than genetic ones. One reason for this is that large changes in the incidence of a disease are seldom attributable to genetics. For instance, the prevalence of obesity has increased dramatically in the last half century. It continues to become more prevalent in the rich parts of the world, and at the same time, it increases in low-and middle-income countries, even in countries where other parts of the population suffer from food shortages and malnutrition.[19] Worldwide obesity has almost tripled since 1975, and more than 650 million adults and more than 100 million children are now obese.[20] There is no way in which this large increase in obesity can be the result of genetic changes – the human genome does not change that fast.[21] Another major reason to focus on environmental factors is that these factors are more access-ible to change than genetic factors.

It has become common to use the term "lifestyle" for some of the living conditions that have an influence on health and disease. Smoking, drug use, and diet are often described as elements of an individual's lifestyle. However, the word "style" is misleading since it creates the impression that we are dealing with something that people can freely and easily choose, just as affluent people can change their fashion style. As almost everyone who has tried to lose weight or stop smoking will know, it is usually no easy matter to change a "lifestyle" that is detrimental to one's health.[22] The term "lifestyle" should therefore be avoided, and preferably replaced by more neutral terms such as "living condi-tions" or "way of life."

3.2 Some Major Preventable Disease Factors

From 1950 to 2017, global life expectancy at birth increased from 53 to 76 years for women and from 48 to 70 years for men. There were increases in all parts of the world but also large regional differences. In the Central African Republic, life expectancy in 2017 was 55 years for women and 49 for men, whereas in Japan it was 87 years for women and 81 for men.[23] It is contested how much different factors have contributed to the increased longevity, but most researchers agree that preventive measures have had a more prominent role than health care improvements. Among the factors mentioned are improved sanitation, clean water, vaccinations, access to antibiotics, insect control, improved access to food, decreased tobacco use, and health services in particu-lar for children.[24] Notably, most of these improvements involve the elimination or reduction of environmental disease-causing factors, whereas none of them concerns genetic factors. Experience shows that environmental and social conditions that contribute to major diseases can be changed in ways that lead to dramatic improvements in public health. There is still much such work that remains to be done.

Table 1. *Some examples of major global causes of death and preventive measures that can substantially reduce mortality. Source: Naghavi et al., 2017.*

Disease / injury	Persons killed per year	Efficient preventive measures
Diarrheal diseases	1.7 million	Sanitation, clean water
Malaria	0.7 million	Mosquito control
Nutritional deficiency	0,4 million	Adequate food supply
Lung cancer	1.7 million	Antismoking measures
Ischaemic heart disease	9.5 million	Antismoking measures and dietary improvement
Chronic obstructive pulmonary disease	2.9 million	Antismoking measures, reductions in air pollution and in exposure to dusts and chemicals
Diabetes mellitus	1.4 million	Healthy diets, exercise
Road injuries	1.3 million	Traffic safety measures

The best estimates of the impact of different factors on the prevalence of severe disease can be found in the Global Burden of Disease studies, which have a strong focus on mortality and its underlying causal factors. These studies show that many of the major causes of death are highly accessible to preventive measures.[25] Table 1 gives some examples of this. Its rightmost column is a list of urgent public health measures.

3.3 Two Perspectives on Disease Causation and Prevention

We can discuss the prevention of disease on two levels: the individual and the population level. The questions we ask on these two levels are different. On the individual level, the main question is usually what can be done to reduce the risk that an individual person contracts the disease. On the population level, the main question is instead what can be done to reduce the incidence of a disease in a population. These questions are not the same, and to answer them we often need to focus on different causal factors. Obesity provides a particularly illustrative example of these differences.

As we noted in Section 3.1, the increased prevalence of obesity cannot be explained by genetic factors, since they do not change that fast. One might think that instead, it should be attributed to a large number of unwise individual decisions that people make about their food and exercise. However, it does not seem credible that our ability to make such decisions has deteriorated that much over the last few decades. There is no plausible reason why a massive and widespread breakdown in individual willpower or decision-making ability should have taken place in this period.[26] Therefore, although nonadherence to good intentions can be a relevant causal factor in discussions on the individual level, it cannot have much of a role when we are looking for explanations of the global trends. In a public health discussion, we will instead have to look for changes in the social conditions under which individuals make their decisions and form their habits.

Obesity results when a person's food energy intake is significantly higher than her energy expenditure. Studies show that increased food energy intake has been the main driver of the obesity epidemic. In high-income countries, the energy expenditure needed in daily life started to decrease already in the early twentieth century, but obesity did not increase until the 1970s. Until then, people ate less – in particular less wheat products – when their energy demand decreased due to less hard labor. The onset of the obesity epidemic coincided in time with an elevated food energy intake.[27] The increased energy intake was triggered by a surge in the sales of ultra-processed food (i.e. food made in industrial processes). Such food typically comes in the form of "ready to eat" or "ready to heat" products for direct consumption. Some common examples are French fries, burgers, sausages, fish nuggets, instant sauces, pies, pizzas, noodles, sweet and salty snacks, sugar-sweetened soft beverages, chocolates, candy (confectionaries), "energy" bars, and ice cream. They are a growing part of the diet. In some high-income countries more than half of the population's total food energy intake is now ultra-processed. Unfortunately, ultra-processed food usually has very poor nutritional qualities. It has high energy density, and is usually high in sugar, salt, and saturated fats, and low in fibers, proteins, and micronutrients. A high intake of ultra-processed food has been shown to be strongly associated with obesity and its concomitant diseases. At least to a large part, this can be explained by the high energy density and low nutritional value of ultra-processed food. The convenience of these products also contributes to overeating. Many of them require no preparation at all, which invites eating at any time and almost any place. Studies show that we tend to eat more when we pay little attention to our eating than when we pay attention to the meal.[28]

One type of ultra-processed food should be mentioned in particular, namely sugar-sweetened soft drinks. In the United States, soft drinks contribute more energy to the diet than any other type of food or beverage. One of the reasons for this is that they are one of the cheapest sources of energy. Several studies show a strong link between soft drinks and obesity. It has been estimated that about a fifth of the net increase in body weight in the United States can be attributed to soft drinks.[29] Other studies show that taxes increasing the price of sugar-sweetened beverages reduce overweight and obesity.[30]

What conclusions can we draw from all this? As already mentioned, the conclusions will differ between the individual and the population level. In a discussion on what an individual can do to avoid developing or worsening obesity, the focus must be on causal factors that the individual can possibly modify. This means that the current food system, with its abundance of cheap and convenient but unhealthy products, has to be taken for granted. An individual strategy against obesity has to navigate within and against that system. This navigation must include means to resist the many unhealthy but immediately gratifying alternatives that will present themselves on a daily basis.

In a strategy to reduce obesity on the population level, the focus must instead be on what we can do to make it easier for us all as individuals to make healthy choices and develop healthy food and exercise habits. That which is taken for granted on the individual level, namely the current food system, must therefore be a central object of change in discussions on the population level. What needs to be done is well-known: healthy food must become cheaper and more easily available, and unhealthy food less promoted. The task responsibilities for these changes in the food system cannot be laid on individual food consumers. They have to be assigned to social agents who have the power and the abilities to carry them through, that is, governments and business companies.

4 The Ethics of Public Health

Living in a human society, rather than as a contactless eremite, gives rise to moral relationships with others who live in that same society. Most basically, we are obliged not to harm each other or expose each other to serious risks.[31] But just not to harm each other is not sufficient for building a good society. We also need to help each other and contribute to joint efforts that benefit us all.

Health is a basic interest of all human beings. Therefore, these basic moral principles pertain very much to issues of health. As members of a human society, we are morally required not to harm or risk each other's health and also to positively support each other's chances of good health.

4.1 Social Contagion

Some ideologists and political philosophers promote an ideal of almost complete individualism, according to which each person fully independently chooses her own way of life. At least as far as health-related behaviors are concerned, this is a completely unrealistic idea. We all depend heavily on the institutions and the social and technological conditions of the society where we live. We also all relate to – and usually follow – the customs, conventions, and habits of that society. Many of these customs and conditions have a considerable impact on our health.

Our individual choices of goods and physical objects are limited by social choices in numerous ways that we seldom reflect upon. Some of these limitations protect our health and safety. If you try to buy a microwave oven that can emit microwaves with the lid open, an electric drill with uncovered live electrical parts, or a car windshield made of common window glass instead of laminated safety glass, you will be disappointed. Such products are not made. In many countries, there are government regulations prohibiting them, but it is highly doubtful whether any manufacturer would start producing them if these regulations were rescinded. These are standards to which we have all become accustomed, and there does not seem to be any opposition to them.

In much the same way, we adjust to the customs and practices that prevail around us, usually without much reflection or conscious decision-making. Most of us dress in about the same way as people around us, and our social interactions and other everyday behaviors conform with the customs and conventions in the societies where we live. These habits appear to us as "natural" and self-evident, and we usually only reflect upon them when we are confronted with other cultures where the traditions are different.

This is no new insight. It has long been known that we humans largely follow the examples of others, both in habits considered to be good and in habits considered to be bad. The importance of this mechanism for shaping human behavior was well recognized among the ancients.[32] The moral virtue of being a good example to others was emphasized for instance by the Confucian philosopher Mengzi (372–289 BCE) and the Christian Church Father John Chrysostom (c. 349–407).[33] The latter's contemporary Julian of Eclanum (c. 386–c. 455) wrote about the danger of following bad examples, the "contagion of sin."[34] Today, there is an extensive literature in social psychology showing that human behavior is to a large extent determined by our tendency to follow the behavior patterns of people around us.[35] The term "social contagion" is often used for this phenomenon.

Eating habits are a prime example. There are large differences between countries, regions, and cultures in what, when, and how we eat, and often also considerable differences between families and smaller communities. Some of these differences have important health implications. For instance, it has been shown that people with obese friends or family members run a higher risk than others to become obese themselves. Possible explanations of these findings are that people are influenced by their friends' eating habits and that friendship with obese persons can change one's norms about the acceptability of overweight.[36]

Other health-related behaviors have also been shown to be socially contagious, including smoking, alcohol consumption, and drug use.[37] Notably, social contagion also has a positive side: health-promoting behavior is facilitated, and more probable, if people in one's close environment have already adopted it. People whose friends and family have managed to cease smoking tend to follow suit, and physical exercise is efficiently encouraged by exercising friends.[38]

Social contagion is equally important for the prevention of accidents that lead to injuries and possibly death. Workers are much more prone to follow safety rules if others in the workplace follow them.[39] In road traffic, "drivers are sensitive to the influence of others and … a small shift in the behavior of few can be amplified, through the interaction between individuals and their collectives, to a larger effect, resulting in a changed social environment or a modified 'culture of driving.'"[40] Drivers have a strong tendency to adapt to the (safe or unsafe) speed at which most other motorists are driving.[41] Similar effects on risky pedestrian behavior have also been shown.[42]

Some safety behaviors are generally taken for granted and are almost ubiquitous. This applies to the use of hard hats on construction sites and seat belts on passenger planes, neither of which seems ever to have been seriously contested.[43] In many countries, both motorcycle helmets and seat belts in cars are approaching the same level of taken-for-grantedness. However, in the Unites States, there is still considerable resistance against motorcycle helmets. Due to political campaigns, many states have revoked laws that made helmets mandatory for all motorcyclists, replacing them with regulations that only require young riders to wear them. Although the law remained the same for young riders, this resulted in a large decrease in their use of helmets. There is no other plausible explanation of this effect than social contagion. Older helmetless riders served as "role models" for young riders – unfortunately with deadly outcomes, since riding helmetless is much more dangerous than riding with a helmet. The number of fatalities among Floridian motorcycle riders below twenty-one nearly tripled after the state allowed older riders to ride helmetless in 2000.[44]

In general, many seemingly individual health-related behaviors are largely shaped by what others do. The other side of this is that each of us influences the people around us in a large number of small ways that we are usually not aware of. If you smoke, then you contribute to normalizing smoking. If you manage to quit smoking, then your success can inspire others to follow your example. If you overeat or drink excessively in other people's company, then that may contribute to normalizing such habits. If you swim in waters where it is forbidden due to dangerous currents, you may contribute to an idealization of daredevil behavior that causes much harm and suffering. If you ride a motorcycle without a helmet, you contribute to creating or maintaining a social environment in which it is normal, perhaps even "tough" or "cool," to risk one's life in this way. On the other hand, if you use a helmet, you contribute to making the use of helmets an unquestioned part of motorcycling, just like the wearing of hard hats on construction sites.

This is a perspective on human behavior that differs much from what we usually encounter in moral philosophy. Modern moral philosophy is dominated by a decision-theoretical approach, in which all morally relevant actions are presumed to be the outcomes of a conscious decision-making process.[45] But that is a misleading picture of the regulation of human behavior. Psychological research shows that many of our behaviors, not least our health-related habits, are enacted without conscious deliberation. Instead, they ensue as automatic responses to environmental cues. As an example of this, what food we eat, and when we stop eating, is mostly a matter of habits or routines that are not accompanied by much conscious reflection.[46] Our automatized habits are so strong that they often override deliberative intentions.[47] Social contagion is a mechanism by which we influence each other's habit formation, without engaging in argumentation or deliberation.

4.2 Our Responsibilities for the Health of Others

Perhaps the most obvious health-related obligation that we have to others is not to infect them with nontrivial infectious diseases. This is why it is a moral obligation to comply with medically justified measures that reduce the risk of contracting and spreading contagious diseases. Literally billions of people have done so during the COVID-19 pandemic, for instance by avoiding crowds, staying at home, keeping distance, and wearing masks.

It is not only for your own sake that you should avoid contracting an infectious disease. Even if you do not worry, or perhaps belong to a group that is almost never severely affected by the particular disease, contracting it is the first condition for spreading it to others – including people who can be much more severely affected. A failure to understand this can be called the *Bolsonaro fallacy* after the Brazilian president Jair Bolsonaro, who flagrantly violated his own administration's COVID-19 regulations, with the justification, "If I have got myself infected, so OK? Look, that is my responsibility, no one has anything to do with this."[48]

The ethical situation is similar for vaccinations against infectious diseases. In general, there are two sufficient reasons to take a vaccine (unless you have a medical contraindication): the vaccine protects your own health, and it also protects others, since if you do not contract the disease you will not spread it.

Therefore, vaccination is not just a personal matter. It is part of a joint effort by which we all contribute to protecting each other.[49]

There are close similarities between infectious contagion and the social contagion that we discussed in Section 4.1. In both cases, the best protection is obtained when the vast majority complies with the protective measures, thereby all contributing to making this the socially normal thing to do. The reason why newcomers on building sites ungrudgingly take up the habit of wearing a hard hat is of course that they see everyone else on the site doing the same. The same mechanism upholds the use of seat belts and motorcycle helmets, and it makes us follow traffic rules and adhere to safety regulations in workplaces.

Both for infectious and social contagion, many small effects can add up to a large and decisive effect. Whether you take the vaccine or not will usually make only a small difference for any particular other person's risk of contracting the disease. Nevertheless, if everyone who can take the vaccine does so, then the number of infected persons will be drastically reduced. One of the best examples of this is measles, a deadly and highly contagious disease. Worldwide vaccination programs have reduced the death toll of this disease from two million per year to less than 100,000 per year. Most of the remaining deaths occur in African countries with a low vaccination coverage. Regions in the world with a high vaccination rate are only affected to a much smaller degree.[50] The sum of many small effects, namely the effects of each person's vaccination, stops the spread of the disease. In the same way, social contagion becomes highly effective when the coverage is large. This applies for instance to the use of motorcycle helmets. In countries like Sweden, the use of these helmets is virtually universal. Young people may never have seen an unhelmeted motorcyclist driving on the road. Using a helmet is the normal thing to do, and the question of riding helmetless will usually not arise. A motorcyclist who breaks this pattern by riding helmetless cannot reasonably claim that this is a matter that only concerns herself. Social contagion is just as real, and can be just as unavoidable, as infectious contagion.

But does social contagion have any moral relevance? Is it at all reasonable to discuss it in moral terms? Someone might retort that these effects on other people's behavior are so small that they can reasonably be neglected. It is true that in most cases, the influence of your example on each person who notices it will be very small. (The major exception is, of course, the influence that parents have on their children.) However, although these influences are small, they are so many that their sum can have a large impact. All of us exert a large number of small influences on a large number of persons, and the sum of all these influences is formidable. It is the force that keeps up traditions, customs, and ways of life on all levels in society. Therefore, the moral relevance of social contagion is beyond doubt. The remaining question is whether we as individuals have any obligations or responsibilities pertaining to our contributions to this powerful social force.

Again, a comparison with infectious contagion is clarifying. It certainly makes a moral difference if a country's population is vaccinated against measles. Compared to a situation with no or insufficient vaccination, a high degree of vaccination will save thousands of children from suffering and possibly death. Each individual vaccination contributes to the large positive moral value of a high vaccination coverage. Since the high coverage is nothing else than the sum of all the individual vaccinations, it would be difficult to deny that these individual vaccinations also have positive moral value. The same argument can be made about social contagion. Everyone who carries a motorcycle helmet contributes to establishing or maintaining a practice that reduces the number of deaths and severe fatalities. Since this practice has a positive moral value, so do the parts of which it consists, that is, the individual acts of helmet-wearing.

An interesting parallel can be drawn with environmental ethics, another area where the sum of many small effects is often morally important. For an example, consider someone who flushes half a bottle of paint thinner down the toilet. Presumably, most of us would morally criticize this action for contributing to environmental pollution. However, there is no harmful effect on the environment that is the consequence of this particular action. This is a common situation when dealing with environmental problems. In particular, nothing I can do makes a noticeable difference to climate change. Nevertheless, it would be a strange view of morality that declared my and everyone else's contributions to these collectively created problems – or to their solutions – to be morally irrelevant.

Unfortunately, standard consequentialist moral theories cannot straightforwardly include this type of small contribution in the moral analysis. (This is because they evaluate an action according to its consequences. On its own, the act of flushing the paint thinner has no negative consequences on the environment.[51]) But fortunately, everyday moral reasoning is better equipped to deal with this type of problem. This is because it contains the age-old principle that one should do one's part in common endeavors. Given the types of problems that we encounter both in environmental policies and in public health, this is an ethical principle that we need more than ever before.

The principle of doing one's part can be straightforwardly applied to each of the three types of issues that we have referred to, namely environmental problems, infectious contagion, and social contagion: Even if none of us makes a noticeable contribution to anthropogenic climate change, the disastrous effects of the sum of our contributions give rise to a joint responsibility for us all to do what we can to reduce greenhouse gas emissions. Similarly, even if the vaccine shots taken by a single person have no observable effects on the spread of the disease, we all have a joint responsibility to contribute to the containment of the disease by taking the vaccine. And even if the social contagion effects of a single person wearing a helmet are too small to be measured, all motorcycle riders have a responsibility to contribute to the large life-saving effect that emerges when the vast majority of them wear a helmet.

4.3 But What About Freedom?

Health and safety measures are far from universally supported. To the contrary, quite a few movements have been formed by opponents of various public health measures. The overarching motto of most of these groups has been freedom or liberty. Tobacco smokers have lobbied for an unfettered freedom to smoke wherever they want.[52] Groups of motorists argue that speed limits infringe on their freedom. And in the COVID-19 pandemic, groups of anti-vaxx, anti-mask, and anti-restriction propagandists have used freedom arguments against regulations and recommendations needed to reduce the spread of this disease.

As these examples all show, those who invoke freedom arguments against public health measures often demand the freedom to engage in behaviors that pose a health risk to others. Passive smoking kills, which is a good reason to make workplaces and public places smoke-free.[53] High speeds on roads increase the risk of deadly accidents.[54] And the fatal effects of refraining from preventive measures against COVID-19 have been demonstrated again and again. Thus these claims to freedom will necessarily have to be weighed against the positive effects of the public health measures in question.

An important distinction has to be made concerning demands of liberty. It can be found for instance in John Stuart Mill's famous book *On Liberty*.[55] He noted that some demands for liberty only affect the person's own interests, not those of other people. Once we have found that a person's claim to a liberty belongs to that category, that is, it affects herself but no one else, we need no more arguments to favor it. All other liberty claims have to be weighed against the interests of other affected persons. In the examples just mentioned, the contrary interests concern considerable risks to life and health. It can certainly not be taken for granted that the liberties to smoke in public places, to drive at high speeds, or to be relieved of infection control measures outweigh an increased number of deaths.

Perhaps surprisingly, very few health-related behaviors belong to the "purely self-regarding" category, those that have no effects on other people. For instance, wearing a seat belt is usually seen as a personal matter, affecting no one else. But in fact, it can have large impacts on others, in particular if you sit in the back seat. According to one study, the risk for a belted driver or front-seat passenger to die in a crash increases almost five-fold if there is an unbelted passenger in the rear seat behind. Therefore the use of seat belts can protect not only the wearer of a belt but also other persons.[56] Many dangerous activities, such as skiing in a place with a high avalanche risk, put rescue workers at risk. Furthermore, if a person is seriously injured or becomes seriously ill, then this can have large consequences for her family and others who depend on her. This is why Mill maintained that "the principal hygienic precepts should be inculcated, not solely or principally as maxims of prudence, but as a matter of duty to others, since by squandering our health we disable ourselves from rendering to our fellow-creatures the services to which they are entitled."[57] If we also take social contagion effects into account, then it will be quite difficult to find examples of health-related behaviors that only have effects on the individual person.

In practice, most if not all public health measures involve different interests that have to be weighed against each other. Such conflicts of interest are often described in terms of "freedom against public health." However, it does not take much reflection to realize that in typical cases, freedoms are involved on both sides in these conflicts. Speed limits restrict the freedom of motorists who prefer to drive faster. But speed limits also reduce the number of severely injured accident victims, whose freedoms of movement and action are reduced for the rest of their lives. Quarantining drastically curtails the freedom of those who are quarantined. But at the same time, it can be an efficient means to protect a large number of people from all the freedom infringements that follow with a serious disease. A prohibition of smoking in public places restricts the freedom of smokers, but it also protects the freedom of nonsmokers. This was recognized already by Mill, who made a brief speech in the British Parliament in 1868 on smoking in railway carriages. He said that "the smoking in trains had become a positive nuisance. Scarcely a railway carriage could be entered in which smoking was not going on, or which was not tainted with stale tobacco." This, in his view, was a case of "oppression by a majority of a minority," the majority being smokers.[58] Thus he gave higher priority to the freedom of nonsmokers not to be disturbed by tobacco smoke than to the freedom of smokers to smoke where they wished to do so. Notably, he and his contemporaries had no knowledge of the severe health effects of smoking.[59] Mill considered the mere nuisance to nonsmokers to be enough to override the smokers' claim to a liberty to smoke.

As Mill also said, "the liberty we stand up for is the equal liberty of all, and not the greatest possible liberty of one, and slavery of all the rest."[60] Liberty for all is a worthy goal. Liberty for oneself at the expense of disease and injuries for others is not.

5 Health Care for All

There could hardly be any more incontestable moral principle than that to the best of our ability, we should relieve the suffering of others. Providing starving people with food is an epitome of a good action, and letting them starve its very opposite. For people with medical needs, access to health care can be just as urgent as food for those who starve. Therefore, the basic principle of relieving suffering requires that to the best of our ability, we should provide health care to those who need it. This is the idea on which the Red Cross and Red Crescent movement and numerous other charities are based. From a moral point of view, all this seems self-evident enough. If we have any moral obligations at all toward our fellow beings, then providing health care to those in need of it should be one of these obligations.

Equally obviously, suffering is not relieved by selling health care at prices that those who need it cannot afford. Arguably, this is equally outrageous as selling food to the starving at extortionate prices. But unfortunately, in countries around the world, mainly low- and medium-income countries, families often find themselves in a position where their only chance to obtain direly needed health care is to take a loan that ruins their economy. According to a WHO estimate based on surveys in a large number of countries, 150 million people each year face catastrophic health care costs, and 100 million are driven below the poverty line.[61] More than 90 percent of those affected by these hardships live in low-income countries. They are usually poor people who have to pay out-of-pocket for each health care service they use, rather than through some prepayment mechanism such as insurance.[62] The same phenomenon can be seen in the United States, where medical bills are still a common cause of economic suffering. In 2014, more than half of the debts sent to debt collection agencies in the United States were medical debts. Although the Affordable Care Act has improved the situation, medical bankruptcy is still a major problem in this country.[63]

Given the basic principle that we should relieve human suffering, it would seem rather self-evident that these hardships have to be abolished. However, the step from a moral standpoint to solving the problem is far from straightforward.

The problem cannot be solved with only individual actions. We need to combine our resources and create systems that offer affordable health care to us all. Almost all industrialized countries have already done so, with important positive effects on the health and general welfare of their populations.[64]

5.1 A Human Rights Perspective

Another ethical perspective on access to health care can be found in international documents on human rights. The most important of these, the Universal Declaration of Human Rights that was adopted by the United Nations General Assembly in 1948, mentions health care as follows in its Article 25:

> Everyone has the right to a standard of living adequate for the health and well-being of himself and of his family, including food, clothing, housing and medical care and necessary social services, and the right to security in the event of unemployment, sickness, disability, widowhood, old age or other lack of livelihood in circumstances beyond his control.[65]

The Declaration does not specify how to achieve that everyone has a sufficient standard to afford the medical care she needs. However, it does not seem to be a realistic interpretation that every person should be rich enough to be able to pay out of pocket for medical treatment even if she contracts a disease that requires a very expensive treatment. A much more realistic way to satisfy the access to health care required in the Declaration is to make sure that medical care is affordable for everyone.

Based on the Declaration of Human Rights, several international human rights treaties have been adopted that give rise to legally binding obligations for governments. One of them is the International Covenant on Economic, Social and Cultural Rights (ICESCR) that was signed in 1966 and came into force in 1976. With its 171 parties, it has almost universal coverage (with the main exception of the United States, which has still not ratified it). Its article 12.2 says:

> The steps to be taken by the States Parties to the present Covenant to achieve the full realization of this right shall include those necessary for: . . .
>   The creation of conditions which would assure to all medical service and medical attention in the event of sickness.[66]

This should be read together with the treaty's second article, according to which each state that is party to the treaty undertakes to take steps "to the maximum of its available resources, with a view to achieving progressively the full realization of the rights recognized in the present Covenant by all appropriate means." This principle of progressive realization expresses a recognition that resource-poor countries cannot immediately achieve universal health care and the other social rights specified in the treaty, but they should still continuously take the steps in that direction that are possible for them.

The Sustainable Development Goals were adopted by the United Nations General Assembly in 2015, with the intention to be achieved in 2030. One of the seventeen goals has its focus on health and includes the following target:

> "Achieve universal health coverage, including financial risk protection, access to quality essential health-care services and access to safe, effective, quality and affordable essential medicines and vaccines for all."[67]

Universal health care coverage is also one of the main goals toward which the World Health Organization (WHO) is working. As WHO defines universal coverage, it means that "all people have access to the health services they need, when and where they need them, without financial hardship."[68] In summary, international declarations and agreements make it a task responsibility for all governments to continuously do what they can to achieve or maintain the goal of affordable health care for all.

5.2 The Introduction of Universal Health Care

The history of health insurance covering those with little means can be traced back at least to the mutual aid societies that were formed by workers in both Britain and France in the eighteenth century.[69] The first national health insurance was introduced in Germany in 1883 by the conservative chancellor Otto von Bismarck. The system was limited to blue-collar workers and their families, about 10 percent of the population. It was funded in part by deductions from wages and in part by fees paid by employers. Coverage was increased in the coming years due to the rapid growth of the industrial sector and to legislation that extended coverage to other groups of employees. In 1914, 37 percent of the population was covered.[70]

The German example was followed by similar legislation in other countries. For instance, in Britain, the National Insurance, introduced by a liberal government in 1911, provided industrial workers with free primary health care. The system was based on contributions from workers themselves (4 pence a week), employers (3 pence a week), and the government (2 pence a week).[71] Similar systems were introduced in country after country, and in the 1930s industrial workers had health insurance in most Western and Central European countries, as well as in Japan and the Soviet Union.

After World War II, these insurance systems were extended to cover the whole population, rather than just industrial workers. This development was pioneered by a Labour government in Britain that introduced a tax-funded universal system in 1948, the National Health Services. It provided free medical services to all according to medical needs rather than ability to pay. This was called the Beveridge system after William Beveridge, whose report on social insurance from 1942 formed the basis of this and other social reforms in Britain. The Beveridge system is often contrasted with the Bismarckian system, which was based on contributions by those ensured and their employers, and therefore did not cover the whole population. Since the 1940s, the countries previously adhering to a Bismarckian system, including Germany where it originated, have gradually extended their health care systems to achieve universal coverage.[72] Today, all the member-states of the European Union, along with industrialized countries in other parts of the world, provide all their citizens with affordable health care. (However, Ireland is struggling with transforming its two-tier system, which provides better health care access to those who can afford private insurance, into a more equitable one-tier system.[73]) Currently, the United States is the only major industrialized country in which a large part of the population still has to pay for medical services out of their own pocket. In spite of the Affordable Care Act, 31.2 million Americans still lack health insurance.[74] This is a considerable improvement since 2006/2007, when nearly 90 million were uninsured, but of course very far from an acceptable situation.[75]

The most remarkable development in access to health care that we have seen in the twenty-first century is that a considerable number of low- and middle-income countries have either achieved or taken large steps toward universal health care coverage. This development disproves a previously widespread belief according to which universal coverage is only possible in rich, industrialized countries. There seem to have been two major arguments for this belief. As economist Amartya Sen has shown, both arguments are based on misconceptions.

The first argument is that universal coverage is much too expensive for low- and middle-income countries. This is an understandable worry. We know how costly health care is in rich countries. Providing every resident in a low-income country with access to health care at anything near these costs would certainly be unrealistic. But this reasoning misses out on a crucial factor, namely that basic health care is a highly labor-intensive activity.[76] Poor countries cannot afford to hire doctors and nurses for their whole population at the salaries that doctors and nurses are paid in high-income countries. However, they can afford to hire doctors and nurses at salaries that are considered reasonable domestically. In this respect, basic health care belongs to the same category as education. If low-income countries had to pay primary school teachers the same salaries as in rich countries, then they would have had no chance to offer all children primary school. But that is not the case, and therefore universal education is feasible even in poor countries. The same is true of universal health care.

The other misconception is that universal health care in poor countries would have to offer the same medical services as in industrialized countries. To the contrary, for people who currently have no access to professional health care, there is typically a large number of diseases that can be cured at low cost.[77] Picking these low-hanging fruits can make a large difference, even if more advanced interventions such as transplantations cannot be offered. Obviously, it would be even better if advanced treatments could also be offered, but there is no reason to delay universal access to the basic treatment of common diseases until more advanced health care can also be offered. Doing so would be about as smart as delaying the introduction of primary school for all children until the country can also offer PhD education at a high international level.

The introduction of universal health care can be seen as an important part of a country's strivings for more equal living conditions among its citizens and residents. However, it is also important to realize that universal health care does not require equality in other respects. A useful approach to the distribution of health care can be derived from the American philosopher Michael Walzer's theory of spheres of justice. According to that theory, different goods have to be distributed according to different principles. Irrespective of how we choose to distribute other goods, health care should be distributed according to medical needs, not according to ability to pay. As Walzer himself pointed out, medical needs can differ a lot between people in the same economic situation. Therefore, general equality cannot solve the problem. "Even with equal incomes, health care delivered through the market would not be responsive to need."[78]

5.3 Achievements in Poor Countries

The ability of poor countries to introduce universal health care is not just a theoretical postulate. There are now quite a few examples of successful reforms in resource-poor countries that have had a large impact on the population's health. One of the most interesting examples is Rwanda, a country that has historically had a dysfunctional health care system. Beginning around the year 2000, the country has systematically improved its health care system and gradually increased its coverage, which is now universal.

The two major systems in the Western world for funding a national health care system are taxes (as in the Beveridge system) and contributions from employers and employees (as in the Bismarckian system). Neither of these systems was suitable for Rwanda, since the formal sector is small, which means that the base for collecting resources in these two ways is too limited. Instead, the country opted for a decentralized system of community-based insurance, known under its French name *mutuelles de santé*. Residents in a locality pay fees to a local health care fund, which pays for their medical treatment when they need it. After pilot projects in three districts, the system was rolled out in 2004 and 2005 to cover the whole nation. Participation was voluntary, and fees were standardized to an amount corresponding to 1.7 USD per year per person. Unfortunately, this was too expensive for a large segment of the population, but that was solved in 2006 through funding from the Global Fund to Fight AIDS, Tuberculosis and Malaria. The Rwandan government made participation in a *mutuelle de santé* compulsory, and the donor paid the fees for the poorest fourth of the population.[79]

For a poor country like Rwanda, international aid was necessary to achieve universal health care coverage. However, the government has avoided what they consider to be an unnecessarily large dependence on foreign donors. In particular, they have rejected proposals from donors to pay the fees of a much larger part of the population, since that would foster long-term dependence on international aid.[80] The government has also considerably increased its own spending on health care.

The Rwandan health care reform has led to a remarkable improvement in the population's health. In one decade, deaths from AIDS, TB, and malaria were reduced by 80 percent.[81] Life expectancy has increased rapidly, from 30 in 1995 (the year after the genocide) to 47.5 in 2000 and 69.1 in 2019.[82] Under-five child mortality has decreased even more dramatically, from 196 per 1,000 live births in 2000 to 34.3 per 1,000 live births in 2019.[83] Rwanda is now often held forth as an example of the successful introduction of universal health care.

Thailand has a similar success story. In the 1990s, only about a quarter of the population had health insurance. The rest of the population had to pay for medical services out-of-pocket on each occasion. About a fifth of the households lived in poverty due to health care spending. In 2001, the government introduced a "30 baht universal coverage program." This meant that no one had to pay more than 30 baht (about US$0.86) for a visit to a health care center. The new health care system was mainly funded by tax revenue, primarily from income tax but also from increased taxes on alcohol and tobacco. The health care reform was generally conceived as successful, and it survived the military coup in 2006.[84] Just as in Rwanda, the effects on the population's health have been dramatic. The under-five mortality rate is now 9 per 1,000 live births, which is fairly close to countries with much more extensive economic resources (e.g., 6.5 in the USA and 4.3 in Great Britain).[85] Life expectancy at birth has risen to 77.7 years, which is quite close to that in some high-income countries (78.5 in the United States and 81.4 in Great Britain).[86] On the 2021 Global

Health Security Index, which measured the preparedness of countries for epidemics and pandemics, Thailand ranked fifth among the 195 evaluated countries and was the only developing country among the top ten.[87]

Comparative studies of low- and middle-income countries introducing universal health care show that they do this incrementally. They typically start with reforms covering less than the whole population and then extend coverage to the rest of the population. They also begin with a limited selection of health care services and gradually add more services. The emerging universal health care systems of these countries do not conform to any of the standard models in Western countries (i.e., neither Beveridge nor Bismarck). Instead, each country develops its own unique funding model, depending on factors such as its previous health care system, its economic structure, and political circumstances affecting support for universal health care. Some countries have managed to integrate private providers and insurers in a new universal system, whereas others have developed a two-tiered system in which those who can afford private insurance have access to service providers that are not available to the rest of the population.[88]

5.4 The Globalization of Health Care

The COVID-19 pandemic should have made it clear that we all depend not only on health care for ourselves but also on health care functioning on the global level. As long as such a disease spreads uncontrolled in some countries, no other country is safe. For epidemiologists, this is not a new insight. The situation is essentially the same for other infectious diseases such as polio, measles, and Ebola. If an outbreak anywhere in the world cannot be controlled, then the disease can spread rapidly to other places. A country or region with insufficient vaccination can become a hotspot from which a disease is transmitted to other countries. Similarly, antibiotic overuse in any part of the world can lead to the development of antibiotic-resistant bacteria that will spread globally and constitute a serious threat to health everywhere.

Someone might object that this can be solved without extending comprehensive health care to everyone on this planet. Is it not sufficient to provide everyone with the necessary vaccinations and introduce strict regulations on the use of antibiotics? No, it does not work that way. In order to get a population vaccinated it is usually not sufficient just to send vaccines or vaccinators with vaccines. The increasing dissemination of disinformation about vaccines makes this more and more difficult.[89] The only reliable way to reach out to a population with vaccination and other preventive measures is through well-established health care centers that are already working with the community. Experiences with Ebola, which has had some of its worst outbreaks in countries and regions with highly insufficient health care resources, show how difficult it is to implement measures such as quarantining and disinfection without a preexisting health care infrastructure. As several authors have pointed out, if the Ebola virus had emerged in a country with a well-functioning health care system, the disease would in all probability have been contained and eliminated at a much earlier stage and with much fewer fatalities.[90] Finally, concerning antibiotic resistance, in order to curb misuse of antibiotics, it is necessary to make these drugs available only after prescription by a medical practitioner. For this to work, all patients potentially needing an antibiotic must have access to a doctor.

Summarizing all this, it should be abundantly clear that it is in everyone's self-interest that the inhabitants of all countries in the world have access to affordable health care services. After a couple of years of experience with COVID-19, it should also be obvious that we all have much to gain if all countries have the capacity to discover and curb new potential pandemics at the earliest possible stage. This means that there are two major reasons for all of us to support universal health care on a global level: the self-interested reason just referred to and the ethical reason that follows directly from the basic principle of relieving the suffering of others. Each of these reasons is in itself sufficient. From an immediate practical point of view, it is not very important which of them is the major driving force, as long as action is taken.

One potential reservation may be that health care for all is too expensive to be realistic. However, calculations performed by the WHO show that it is indeed economically realistic. The best estimate can be found in a research report written for the WHO in 2017, which is based on studies of costs and resources in almost all low- and middle-income countries. It showed that the total cost per year to achieve universal health care in all low- and-middle income countries would be about US$371 billion. Middle-income countries are capable of financing this investment themselves, but low-income countries need support. The total annual need for external assistance is estimated at US$17–35 billion.[91] This is certainly a lot of money, but it can be compared to the total yearly amount of development assistance, US$161 billion, the global yearly sales of cosmetic products, around US$400 billion, or the world's total military spending, US$1,960 billion.[92]

Building health care for all is not only a matter of money. It is also to a high degree a matter of quality of care. Low quality, leading to inadequate treatment, is a severe problem in many low- and middle-income countries.[93] The major means for quality improvement is of course education of health care workers. (We will return to quality of care in the next chapter.) Another serious problem in many health care systems is corruption. It can take many forms, including costly but unnecessary procedures, unauthorized informal payments from patients, theft of drugs and equipment, absenteeism that may be combined with private practice elsewhere, and so forth. Poor countries that lack mechanisms for oversight of government employees are particularly affected. Strict oversight and anticorruption measures are necessary to ensure that funding for universal health care is used for its intended purpose.[94]

To sum up, the basic requirement to relieve suffering implies that we should take responsibility for each other's access to health care. This is essentially a task responsibility; blame responsibility usually has no constructive role to play here. Notably, it is a responsibility that cannot be satisfied just by individual action. It requires cooperation and coordination. We need to act together and make sure that our governments work for us and ensure affordable health care for all residents. Poor countries will need international aid to achieve a universal health care system within a reasonable time. Rich countries have two reasons to provide such assistance: the ethical requirement to relieve suffering and their (self-interested) need for a globally functioning health care infrastructure in which new infectious diseases can be curbed at an early stage wherever they appear.

6 Responsibility in Health Care

Taking care of another person's medical needs means entering a relationship that is very different from other private (or commercial) relationships. In relation to each patient, a physician or nurse undertakes a fiduciary responsibility, a responsibility for acting in the patient's interest as far as her health is concerned.[95] The notion of special responsibilities bound to the role of the physician can be traced back at least to the Hippocratic oath, named after the Greek physician Hippocrates (c. 460–c. 370 BCE). According to this oath, when acting as a professional, a physician had special duties and responsibilities such as to care for the sick, keep information from patients secret, and treat all patients alike, whether they were men or women, rich or poor, free or slaves. If needed, the physician should treat the poor for free. The physician should always serve the ill, and could not undertake to poison a person or tell others how to do so.[96]

These principles are still parts of the ethics of the medical profession. For instance, all major organizations in the medical profession consider it impermissible for their members to contribute in any way to capital punishment.[97] Justifying this standpoint, the American Medical Association has stated that irrespective of the individual physician's private views on capital punishment, "as a member of a profession dedicated to preserving life when there is hope of doing so," a physician should not participate in an execution.[98]

6.1 From Paternalism to Informed Consent

Traditionally, it has been assumed that the doctor knows best and should therefore make the medical decisions, choosing treatment for the patient without giving her much of a say or even an explanation or justification. This model is commonly called "paternalism." It had adherents well into the 1990s.[99] Some proponents even defended it by explicitly comparing the relationship between patient and physician to that between child and parent.[100]

Beginning in the 1950s, the paternalist model was more and more challenged, and within a few decades, it was replaced by the model of informed choice, which puts strong emphasis on the patient's autonomy and self-determination.[101] The physician should inform and advise the patient and propose appropriate diagnostic and therapeutic interventions. However, the patient herself should make the final decisions. This approach is based on the assumption that patients are autonomous individuals, capable of deciding for themselves if provided with the right information. (Exceptions are made for patients who lack decision-making capacity, such as children, unconscious persons, and persons with severe mental disabilities. In these cases, decisions have to be made either by a proxy who knows the patient well or by the medical personnel responsible for the treatment.) In clinical practice, the informed choice model requires the physician to obtain the patient's informed consent before performing an intervention. For the consent to be informed, the patient should have received the relevant information about expected therapeutic effects, side effects and risks, available alternatives, and the uncertainties involved.

The choice of the term "informed consent" rather than for instance "informed decision" tells us something important about what is expected of the patient. This can perhaps best be seen by comparison with how we would use the term "consent" in other contexts.

Consider a rich investor, who instructs her employees to put together and investigate several investment alternatives, closely follows and directs their work, and then after careful consideration orders them to implement one of these alternatives. We would hardly say that she "consented" to how her money was invested. This is because she did much more than consent, namely oversaw and controlled the whole decision-making process. The term "consent" would be more appropriate in the case of a small saver who authorizes a bank official to do as the latter proposes.

A patient giving informed consent to a surgical procedure is in a situation much more similar to that of the small saver than the rich investor in this example. She has either accepted the surgeon's only proposal as the best option or made a choice among a few therapy options that have been proposed to her. This is by no means inappropriate. It would not be realistic for patients to take part in the medical deliberations leading up to the treatment proposals.

In the informed choice model, the physician is the patient's advisor, tasked with proposing and explaining treatment alternatives, and advising her choice. However, the physician's role goes beyond that of merely advising. This is because medical ethics contains the principles of nonmaleficence and beneficence, both of which are essential for safeguarding treatment quality and patient safety.[102] According to the principle of beneficence, patients should only be offered medically beneficial treatments. The principle of nonmaleficence specifically disallows treatments whose expected effects are predominantly harmful. Due to these principles, the physician is responsible for offering as beneficial treatments as possible and for not harming the patient. The injunction against harmful treatments cannot be overridden by the patient's consent, not even if the patient actively asks for the treatment. For instance, a patient whose heart condition contraindicates sildenafil (which can cure erectile dysfunction) should not receive a prescription for this medicine, even if he expresses a strong wish for it.

Another way to express this is that two requirements have to be satisfied for an intervention on a patient to be ethically acceptable. One of these requirements is the patient's informed consent (with the above-mentioned exception for patients who are temporarily or permanently incapable of giving or withholding consent). The other requirement is that according to the best available information, the intervention is beneficial for the patient's health. Both these requirements are necessary conditions for ethical acceptability, but neither of them is sufficient. Seen from the negative side, it is unethical to administer a beneficial treatment to a (decision-capable) person who did not consent to it, and it is also unethical to administer a harmful intervention to a patient even if she has consented to it.

Some authors have proposed that by letting patients choose treatments, physicians can protect themselves against malpractice litigation. "By sharing more and more responsibility with patients, physicians can free themselves from some of the responsibility for unwise decisions or unfavorable outcomes."[103] However, this can only happen if the law fails to recognize the principles of beneficence and nonmaleficence, which disallow harmful interventions.

To sum up, the informed choice model of the patient-physician relationship, which dominates in today's health care, assigns responsibilities to both patients and physicians. However, these responsibilities are very different in nature. The physician is responsible for offering the patient the best possible treatment alternative(s) and, if needed, other beneficial alternatives that are more compatible with the patient's values. She is also responsible for administering the beneficial treatment to which the patient gives informed consent. The patient is responsible for her own informed choices, in the sense that if she was adequately informed, then she cannot legitimately blame the physician for not having made another choice. Since these responsibilities are different in nature, it is not quite adequate to describe the patient and the physician as having a "joint" or "shared" responsibility for the choice of a treatment. They can perhaps better be described as having separate responsibilities pertaining to one and the same decision.

6.2 Finding the Best Treatment

We just noted that one of a physician's primary responsibilities is to recommend the best available treatment for the patient's disease. In order to further specify that responsibility, and to distinguish it from other responsibilities that are shared within the profession, we need to have a close look at how the effects of treatments can be determined.

There is indeed a superior method to determine and compare both the positive and the negative effects of different treatments, namely to systematically test these treatments on patients with the disease in question and carefully record both positive and negative effects on each patient. In spite of its simplicity, this method was developed and put to general use surprisingly late in history. One of the most famous early treatment experiments was performed in 1747 by the Scottish naval surgeon James Lind (1716–1794). He divided twelve sailors afflicted by scurvy into six groups of two. Each of the six groups received a different treatment: cider, a weak acid, vinegar, seawater, nutmeg and barley water, or oranges and lemons. After six days, the two men on a citrus treatment had regained health, whereas all the others remained sick.[104]

Another interesting early treatment experiment was performed by the Polish-Austrian physician Joseph Dietl (1804–1878) in the late 1840s. At that time, the general view among physicians was that pneumonia depends on an imbalance between bodily fluids. They all tried to cure the disease by restoring that balance, but there were two major theories on how this should be done. Most physicians recommended blood-letting, but some favored the administration of emetics (substances causing vomiting). In 1849, Dietl reported an investigation in which he compared three groups of pneumonia patients. One group had received blood-letting, the second an emetic, and the third general care but no specific treatment. Mortality among those who had received blood-letting was 20.4 percent, among those who had received an emetic 20.7 percent, and among those who had received no specific treatment only 7.4 percent. This, of course, implied that neither of the two traditional treatments should be used. The traditional treatments were gradually abandoned, and in the 1870s the major medical textbooks advised against blood-letting of pneumonia patients.[105]

One may well ask: How could the doctors be so wrong? How could the majority of physicians perform blood-letting on their pneumonia patients, without noticing that this treatment worsened rather than improved the patient's condition? The answer is that they were victims of a very general weakness in human cognition. Once you start to believe that something you do has certain effects, you tend to interpret what you observe as more supportive of this belief than what it really is. Pneumonia, in particular, is a disease in which a patient's status often fluctuates (goes up and down). If a patient's health improved a bit after a session of blood-letting, then this was interpreted as a sign that the treatment had a positive effect. On the other hand, if her condition worsened after blood-letting, then this was taken to show that more of the same was needed. If her condition improved somewhat after an additional blood-letting, then that was interpreted as a positive treatment effect. This is a faulty way of reasoning that affects not only physicians but also the rest of us. For instance, it explains why so many ineffective household remedies have unswerving adherents. Once you start to believe that tea with honey – or something else – shortens a cold, you will tend to interpret your experiences as confirmations of that belief.

More generally, unsystematized practical experience is much less reliable than what we would like to believe. Unless treatment effects are dramatic, they cannot be verified by just observing and remembering the effects. We need to do as Joseph Dietl did, namely perform a planned test of the alternative treatments we want to evaluate, and carefully record and count all the outcomes.

Lind's and Dietl's studies were rare exceptions. Well into the twentieth century, very few treatment experiments were made. Case reports covering one or a few patients were much more common in the medical literature than methodical comparisons between different treatments. It was not until after World War II that experimental comparisons of drugs and other treatments gained traction in the medical world. But in the last half of the twentieth century, the standards of medical evidence underwent dramatic changes. The methodology of treatment experiments, or clinical trials as they are commonly called, was considerably sharpened in order to make the results more reliable. In order to avoid selection bias, patients had to be randomized between treatment groups. In order to avoid other types of bias, neither patients nor the physicians evaluating the effects on their health were allowed to know which of the alternative treatments the patient received (double-blind testing). Furthermore, systematic methods have been developed to combine information from several clinical trials of the same treatment. These methods have a central role in evidence-based medicine, medical practice based on the systematic evaluation of the therapeutic and adverse effects of treatments.

Clinical trials belong to a special group of experiments, namely directly action-guiding experiments.[106] By this is meant experimental tests of some practical method in order to determine if that method works. Action-guiding experiments can also be found in agriculture and technology. Farmers and agricultural scientists compare different seeds or cultivation methods by using them on adjacent fields under similar conditions. Such experiments are called field trials. Engineers try out new constructions in order to determine whether they work. The different types of action-guiding experiments, including clinical trials, are all based on a very simple principle:

> If you want to know if you can achieve Y by doing X, then do X and see if Y occurs.

For statistical effects, this recipe has to be somewhat elaborated:

> If you want to know if you can make Y more probable by doing X, then do X many times under similar circumstances and see if Y becomes more common.

These recipes are in a sense self-vindicating. For instance, if you want to know if oranges cure scurvy, what better method can there be than to give oranges to a group of patients with scurvy and compare them to patients who are not served any oranges?

Thus clinical trials provide much of the information needed for the choice of treatments. However, they also have limitations. Perhaps most importantly, although clinical trials inform us of the effects of different treatments, they do not tell us how to value these effects. In particular, they do not tell us how to weigh therapeutic effects against adverse effects or how much importance to attach to rare but serious adverse effects. These are value judgments, not scientific issues. Fortunately, the vast majority of people tend to make most such judgments in a fairly similar way. If told what effects different treatments have, we usually agree on which has the best balance of therapeutic effects versus adverse effects. This conformity of human judgment much facilitates the physician's task of recommending patients treatments against their disease.

But although this holds in most cases, there are also notable exceptions. Depending on their life situation and life plans, patients differ widely in their appraisals of infertility as a side effect of a treatment.[107] Breast cancer patients who were told that the risk of cancer recurrence was smaller with radical mastectomy than breast reconstruction made different choices based on that information.[108] Similarly, some but not all women with a genetically enhanced risk of breast cancer choose preventive mastectomy to avoid the disease.[109] In such cases, it is necessary to combine information obtained from clinical trials with information on the patient's values. But the need for such deliberations does not reduce the need for accurate information about the therapeutic and adverse effects of the treatment(s) under consideration. (For instance, exactly what effects do the different types of breast operations have on the risk of breast cancer?) If well-conducted clinical trials have been performed, then they provide the best information about positive and negative treatment effects. Therefore, a positive therapeutic effect shown in clinical trials, not outweighed by uncontroversially worse adverse effects, should be seen as a minimal criterion for clinical use. In other words, it should be seen as a necessary but not sufficient requirement for a treatment to be routinely offered to patients.

Clinical trials also have another important limitation: They can tell us *if* a treatment works or not (relative to our chosen criteria), but they do not tell us anything about *how* it works. For instance, a drug's mechanism of action cannot be inferred from clinical trials. From the viewpoint of practical medicine, this is usually no great problem. In order to offer patients a drug or some other therapy, it is not necessary to know *how* it works, as long as one knows *that* it works. However, mechanistic understanding is essential in medical research. In order to improve a drug or replace it with something better, researchers need to know its mechanism of action in as much detail as possible.

6.3 Personal and Collegial Responsibilities

It follows from all this that the general assessment of treatment alternatives for various diseases is not a personal issue for the individual physician. We do not expect a general practitioner to study the research literature on all the diseases that she encounters in her practice. These assessments are a collegial, not a personal responsibility. Like many other collegial tasks, it involves a considerable division of labor, such that specialists in a particular area jointly take charge of the treatment evaluations in that area. This is a task responsibility seldom associated with much blame responsibility. Improved treatment recommendations are usually promulgated with reference to new research, without any discussion of whether anyone is to blame for the deficiencies in the old recommendations.

But nevertheless, physicians are still personally responsible for their diagnoses and treatments of individual patients. Thus, whereas general principles for the treatment of various diseases are a collegial task responsibility, it is a personal responsibility for the physician to propose an adequate treatment to each individual patient, based on these general principles and her knowledge about the patient. One part of this responsibility is to be aware of the limitations of one's own knowledge and to consult with colleagues in other specialties whenever needed.

Contrary to the collegial responsibility just referred to, a physician's personal responsibility for the treatment of her patients involves both blame and task responsibility. A physician who has administered an inefficient, perhaps even harmful, treatment is considered blameworthy, not only morally but in many cases also by the legal system. In some countries, physicians run a considerable risk of litigation for allegedly erroneous diagnoses or treatments.

As we saw in Section 2.2, experience from other areas shows that a strong focus on blame for individual failures can stand in the way of efficient measures to prevent future adverse events. Occupational safety improved when the focus shifted from mistakes by individual workers to the creation of workplaces where such mistakes do not have catastrophic consequences. Similarly, traffic safety has improved through the creation of safer roads and vehicles. Previous attempts to make drivers drive safely in an unsafe traffic system were not effective. Is the situation similar in health care?

We cannot completely dispense with blame responsibility for individual mistakes. There are practitioners who repeatedly make serious mistakes due to incompetence or carelessness. In incorrigible cases, there is no other solution than to withdraw their license, just as incorrigibly dangerous drivers lose their driving license. But these individuals are few. Most of the harmful events in health care originate in rare errors made by physicians and nurses who otherwise do a good job. Just as any worker in a mechanical workshop can put her hand where it should not be, any physician or nurse can make a mistake. To improve patient safety, it is therefore necessary to look for deficiencies in routines, equipment, and other components of the health care system.

A Swedish case from 2002 serves unusually well to illustrate the problem. In that year, a three-month-old baby died in a hospital in Kalmar after receiving a ten times too high concentration of an intravenously administered drug. The nurse who had prepared the infusion was indicted and sentenced for involuntary manslaughter. An investigation of the event revealed several deficiencies in the medication routines. A major causal factor was that the packages of this drug with 20 mg/ml and 200 mg/l were very similar. The nurse was accustomed to packages with the first of these concentrations and did not notice the difference. One of the most basic measures to decrease the risk of dosage mistakes is to make packages with different concentrations of a drug conspicuously different. This case gave rise to a considerable debate, in which many questioned why the nurse had to carry the whole blame responsibility. Critics also pointed out that task responsibilities for avoiding similar mistakes had a remarkably small role in the official reactions to the accident.[110]

Experts on patient safety have since long proposed that health care organizations should tone down the previously dominant culture of blame and instead develop a safety culture that sees errors and incidents as system problems for the organization as a whole to deal with.[111] Many health care institutions around the world have taken important steps in that direction. They encourage employees to bring up all concerns about patient safety.[112] They have also introduced programs of continuous improvement, focusing on the construction and implementation of practices that reduce both the risk of medical failures and the consequences of such failures.[113] These developments have led to a shift in discussions on professional responsibility in health care, from individual blame responsibility to collective task responsibilities.

6.4 Uneducated Practitioners

Up to now, we have discussed the responsibilities of persons belonging to an established health care profession, such as those of physicians and nurses. Do the same principles apply to laypersons who lack the education required for entering these professions but still offer treatments to persons seeking their help? The answer to that question is straightforward once we recognize that patients go to see practitioners without a medical education with the same expectations as when they consult doctors or nurses: to obtain the best possible treatment for their condition. A person who offers health care services is responsible for meeting this expectation to the best of her ability. Offering patients a worse treatment than they could otherwise have received means to betray them and not to meet this responsibility.

It is important to distinguish between two groups of health care practitioners lacking a physician or nurse licensure. One group consists of the many practitioners lacking formal education and license who work in the health care systems of low-income countries with too few doctors and nurses to fill the positions that need to be filled. Many of these practitioners do a fairly good job, and the health care system in these countries could not do without them.[114] Their ability to fulfill their responsibilities towards patients can be significantly improved by offering them training and making it possible for them to refer patients to trained personnel.[115] The ultimate goal for a country's health care system should of course be that all practitioners have a full professional education and a license to practice.

Not least in high-income countries, there is also another group of unlicensed health care providers, namely those who offer their patients treatments for which there is no evidence of any positive effects, such as homeopathy, naturopathy, and a large number of unproved herbal remedies.[116] Telling patients that alleged cures are provenly effective although they are not is a breach of every health care provider's responsibility to offer one's patients the best available treatment.

6.5 Artificial Intelligence[117]

Health care is one of the sectors where the use of artificial intelligence (AI) has advanced most rapidly. In some areas of medical image processing, artificial intelligence systems already outperform human specialists.[118] This has given rise to at least three important questions related to the responsibility for decision-making in health care.[119] First, will machines and algorithms take over to such an extent that we will have to assign (blame and task) responsibility to the AI itself, rather than to some human designer or user of it (the question of responsible AI)? Secondly, will there be issues for which neither humans nor the AI can be assigned responsibility (the question of responsibility gaps)?[120] And thirdly, will ascriptions of blame and task responsibility be obstructed by our inability to understand the conclusions offered by artificial intelligence (the question of explainability)?

Concerning the first question, it is important to distinguish between two distinct versions of the question:[121]

> A: Will we have reasons to assign (blame or task) responsibility to any future AI application?
> B: Will we have reasons to assign (blame or task) responsibility to any of the AI applications that are currently used, or will foreseeably be used, in health care?

Version A of the question can only be answered tentatively, since the answer depends on what types of artificial intelligence humans will encounter in the future. Perhaps future artificial intelligences will exhibit beliefs and desires, and communicate with humans about moral issues just like we communicate with each other. Then humans may be disposed to assign both blame and task responsibilities to these artificial agents. However, it is much less plausible that we will assign responsibilities to more task-limited artificial agents that have been constructed to perform specific tasks in response to orders given to them by humans.[122] In version B of the question, we are concerned with agents of the latter type. There will be no reason to make programs for specific medical tasks emulate general human beliefs, desires, or morality. Therefore, they are not plausible candidates for being treated as responsible agents. In all probability, we will treat the responsibility issues for these artificial agents in the same way as we do for other technological artifacts (including self-driving cars): we will distribute these responsibilities among the humans who construct the artifacts, create the systems in which they are used, and operate them within these systems.

Our second question, about responsibility gaps, can be answered very much in the same vein. In order for responsibility gaps to arise, there must be automated systems that we consider to be so out of human control that we cannot assign responsibility for what they do either to their designers or to their owners and users. It is possible that such systems will be created in the future. However, the AI systems to be introduced in health care in the foreseeable future will have strictly delimited tasks that they perform in response to human orders. Therefore we have no reason to believe that they will give rise to responsibility gaps.

Our third question, about explainability, may need some further clarification. There are two major forms of AI. The oldest form is often called an expert system. It contains a database of rules that have been encoded from the knowledge of human experts. If the encoding was successful, then the outcomes of the system will coincide with what human experts would have concluded, and can then also be understood and explained by these experts. The other version of AI is machine learning. It takes the form of programs (algorithms) that do not contain any rules for the particular subject matter, but instead rules for learning from a large database of information. For instance, the program may have access to a large number of medical images of some organ, each combined with the final diagnosis that the patient received. The program can use this information to systematically search for early signs of various diseases in the organ in question. In this case, a question of explainability can arise since human experts may not be able to figure out what cues the machine makes use of.

Like all other important new health care technologies, those based on artificial intelligence will have to be evaluated according to the criteria of evidence-based medicine. For instance, if trials confirm that an image-processing program discovers signs of a disease on X-ray images at an earlier stage than most human radiologists, then this is a good reason to use that program. The crucial issue here is whether it really delivers the desired result, not whether or not we understand how it does so. This is just one more implication of the basic insight, described in Section 6.2, that the essential criterion for using a method in health care is confirmation *that* it works, not understanding of *how* it works. Many drugs with unknown mechanisms are used in health care, for the simple reason that there is sufficient evidence that they actually work.[123] For similar reasons, it need not be a problem that we do not understand how an AI technology arrives at a particular diagnosis or treatment recommendation. What we need to know is that treatments based on its outputs yield the desired results. Just like other medical technologies, AI applications can be used if they have been shown to produce satisfactory results, even if the question "how" has not yet been answered. Issues of responsibility for the use of medical technology will continue to concern whether or not it works, not whether or not its mode of action is well understood.

7 Responsibility for One's Own Health

Finally, we will turn to what is probably the most discussed issue on responsibility in health care, namely the responsibility that each of us has for our own health. Aren't we responsible for leading a healthy life? If illness befalls us, aren't we responsible for following the instructions of health care professionals in order to get better? And what are the implications if we fail to comply with these responsibilities?

7.1 A Divided Practice for Patient Responsibility

To answer these questions we need to – again – distinguish between blame and task responsibilities. There cannot be much doubt that we all have task responsibilities for our own health. In health care, most consultations end up with recommendations for the patient to follow. Patients are advised to take medicines, stop smoking, reduce their alcohol consumption, engage in physical activity, perform specific exercises, change their diets, and so forth. This means that task responsibility for these interventions is laid on the patient.[124] The reason for this is trivial: no one else can do it.

When it comes to blame responsibility, the tradition in health care is quite different. In their encounters with patients, health care professionals tend to apply a well-developed but seldom discussed *divided practice for patient responsibility*: They assign task responsibilities but avoid assigning blame responsibility even if a patient fails to fulfill her task responsibilities. This is a practice that lacks documentation, and it has only rarely been explicitly articulated and analyzed. We can describe it as tacit knowledge in the health care professions.[125] Briefly, the practice can be summarized as follows: Patients are assigned task responsibilities concerning all the factors in health care that they are themselves best suited to do anything about. If successful, they are often praised for their achievements, in particular if the task was a difficult one such as giving up smoking. However, if a patient fails in some of these tasks, she is seldom blamed for her failure. Instead of being burdened with blame responsibility for not following the advice, she is offered support for new attempts to do so. For instance, a patient who did not manage to stop smoking will usually not be reprehended by her physician or told that it is now her own fault if she has a heart attack. Instead, she will be offered new help, for instance nicotine patches or participation in a smoking cessation program.

There are strong medical and ethical justifications for this practice. To begin with, many health-promoting changes in our ways of life are quite difficult to carry through. We have all failed on occasion to follow through with our good intentions, and many of us have experienced that both hunger and nicotine urges can be overwhelming and almost impossible to resist. A physician who recommends a patient to change her diet or stop smoking cannot know how difficult this will be for the person in question. However, there are good reasons to assume that people for whom it is exceptionally difficult to carry through these recommendations are overrepresented among those who do not succeed in following them. A patient who failed to change her habits may have tried much harder, and endured more hardship during her attempts, than most of those who succeeded. It would then be unfair to blame her for the failure.

Furthermore, studies show that blaming a person is often counterproductive. Blame tends to incite feelings of guilt. Such feelings add to suffering and tend to hamper rather than stimulate health-promoting behavior. For instance, obese patients who have been exposed to stigmatization and blaming are usually less successful than other patients in losing weight.[126] Among people suffering from alcohol use disorders, those who feel stigmatized are less likely than others to follow the treatment programs they are offered.[127] Other studies confirm that self-blame aggravates the suffering of patients with a wide range of diseases.[128] People who blame themselves for a disease and attribute it to their own behavior also run an increased risk of negative mental health outcomes such as depression.[129] All this gives health care workers good reasons to communicate with patients in ways that as far as possible reduce the risk of inducing self-blame. The divided practice for patient responsibility is a way to achieve this.

7.2 Blame-Based Treatment Denial

In the 1960s, definitive evidence of the severe health effects of smoking became available and was widely publicized. Since then, knowledge about the connections between human disease and behavioral factors such as smoking, diet, insufficient exercise, and so forth has led to extensive health-promoting measures. Some of these measures, in particular those against smoking, have been highly successful. For instance, about eight million premature deaths were prevented by tobacco control measures in the United States between 1964 and 2012.[130]

In particular since the 1990s, knowledge about these behavioral factors has also led to proposals for a very different type of policy measures: it has been suggested that the victims of diseases related to tobacco, alcohol, and obesity should be deprived of publicly funded health care. For instance, it has been proposed that persons with smoking-related diseases should be excluded from insurance coverage for these diseases and that, for moral reasons, alcoholics should have lower priority than others for liver transplantation.[131] Proposals have also been made that publicly funded health services should stop offering obese people expensive treatments, a measure that would allegedly "shock a huge number of the overweight into taking responsibility for their own condition."[132] The general idea behind these proposals is that patients who caused their own disease have thereby forfeited the right to publicly funded health care.

In politics, blame-based treatment denial is particularly popular among conservatives.[133] In contrast, most of the ethicists and philosophers who support such policies call themselves "luck egalitarians," a designation indicating that blame-based treatment denial would in some way contribute to creating a more equal society.[134] The notion of "luck egalitarianism" relies heavily on Ronald Dworkin's distinction between option luck and brute luck. Option luck depends on the individual's own choices. It is "a matter of how deliberate and calculated gambles turn out – whether someone gains or loses through accepting an isolated risk he or she should have anticipated and might have declined," in other words the outcome of the individual's own risk-taking. Brute luck is the fallout of risks that "are not in that sense deliberate gambles."[135] According to "luck egalitarianism," society should compensate individuals for misfortunes caused by brute luck but not for misfortunes that are "in some way traceable to the individual's choices."[136] In practice, luck egalitarians have targeted the same medical conditions as conservative proponents of blame-based treatment denial, namely the major "lifestyle" diseases associated with smoking, alcohol, drugs, and obesity.

For "luck egalitarianism" to be at all plausible, there must be some kind of moral link from the sick person's choices (and option luck) to a justification for denying her publicly funded medical treatment that she would otherwise have been offered. This link is usually taken to be one of responsibility. According to "luck egalitarians," we should be held blame responsible for diseases caused by our own choices.[137] However, as we saw in the previous section, holding people (blame) responsible for their disease aggravates their suffering and tends to make it more difficult for them to follow health-promoting recommendations.

The assignment of blame for "lifestyle" diseases is also problematic from another point of view, namely the stochastic nature of disease causality. Although factors such as smoking, alcohol dependence, and obesity lead to rather dramatic increases in the risks of many diseases, those diseases are not exclusively connected with these factors. For instance, the probability that a nonsmoker contracts lung cancer is between 1/30 and 1/15 of the probability that a smoker does so. For some cancers, a nonsmoker has about 2/3 of the risk that a smoker has.[138] Therefore, it is impossible to determine whether a particular smoker who contracted cancer would also have contracted this disease if she had not smoked. On the group level, we know for sure (that is, beyond reasonable doubt) that smoking causes a large number of cancers, but on the individual level, causality cannot be known for sure. The same applies to other "lifestyle" factors: for a non-obese person the risk of type 2 diabetes (adult-onset diabetes) is between 1/12 and 1/8 of the corresponding risk for a person with severe obesity.[139]

Notably, the proposals to refuse public funding for the treatment of diseases caused by smoking and obesity are based on the assumption that the causal connection between habits and disease can be safely determined. The fact that this cannot be done is no small matter, considering what is at stake. Denying someone medical treatment can have serious, even lethal consequences. This is why denial of treatment is commonly considered to be a cruel and unusual punishment.[140] Remarkably, no proponent of blame-based treatment denial seems to have proposed legal procedures that would guarantee basic rule-of-law principles, such as the accused's right to be presumed not to have caused her own disease, unless and until it has been established beyond reasonable doubt that she has done so. Instead, it seems to be taken for granted that these decisions should be made by physicians. This, however, would be "punishment without a hearing or trial by individuals who were effectively jury, judge, and execu-tioner rolled into one."[141] Physicians have no education for any of these roles, and the idea of letting one person fill all the roles is a legal monstrosity.[142] This would be unacceptable in a legal procedure where only a small fine was at stake. It should certainly not be accepted when a person's access to health care is in question.

Tasking physicians with decisions to deny health care would also severely damage the traditional fiduciary relationship between patients and physicians. In that relationship, it is in the patient's interest not to withhold any information and to answer the physician's questions truthfully. In a system with blame-based treatment denial, this would be very different.[143] A patient could try to make herself eligible for expensive cardiac surgery by claiming to have started to smoke only very recently. A patient with hepatitis could choose to withhold the information that she has previously injected drugs, in order not to be excluded from any treatment option. After blame-based treatment denial has been introduced, it would probably not take long before extensive information could be found on the internet about what one should say and not say to one's doctor in order not to be denied treatment.

7.3 Three Issues of Fairness

Blame-based treatment denial gives rise to at least three quite problematic issues of fairness.

First, the statement that a disease is caused by a person's own decisions does not necessarily say all that we need to know about the moral worth of those decisions. Proponents of treatment denial tend to only consider decisions that induce a disease and bring nothing morally valuable with them. However, not all health-damaging choices are of that nature. Consider a person who has spent the last twenty years working around the clock for an NGO that helps dissenters in dictatorships to escape to freedom. Thanks to her work, hundreds of political refugees have been able to leave a country where many of them would otherwise have been detained for decades in overcrowded prisons. However, she has not had time for physical exercise, and she has ordered most of her meals from a nearby fast-food restaurant. She is now severely obese. Should she be denied treatment along with all the obese people who have no such mitigating circumstances?

And what about a physician or nurse who volunteered to care for patients with a contagious deadly disease and was herself infected? Her disease is certainly traceable to her own (option luck) decisions. Should she therefore be denied treatment? No protests were heard when physicians and nurses who contracted Ebola when working as volunteers in West Africa were evacuated in expensive transatlantic ambulance flights to American hospitals.[144]

Examples like these show that in practice, a system of blame-based treatment denial would have to make exceptions for persons whose unhealthy choices are considered to be praiseworthy. This means that procedures for evaluating the worthiness of people's life choices would have to be introduced. But do we want this type of institutionalized moralizing?

Secondly, it appears both strange and disproportionate to withdraw medical treatment from people who have mismanaged their own health, while people who have done much worse things receive all the treatments they need. There are quite a few "blameworthy individuals including convicted criminals that have committed much more heinous crimes than repeatedly picking the wrong dessert."[145] For instance, compare the following two persons: One is a nursing assistant who does excellent work for her patients but mismanages her own health by smoking several packages of cigarettes every day. She has contracted ischaemic heart disease, which her physicians attribute to her smoking. The other person is the CEO of a tobacco company. Thousands of people have died from the products marketed by his company. However, he has always led a very healthy life, and he has never smoked. In spite of this, he has also contracted ischaemic heart disease. According to proponents of blame-based treatment denial, the nursing assistant but not the CEO has a self-inflicted disease and can therefore be denied treatment. How fair is that?

Thirdly, and in my view most importantly, blame-based treatment denial will in practice only affect the poor, not the rich. Proponents of treatment denial have only proposed limitations in the health care that is paid with public means, such as taxes and obligatory insurance premiums. No one seems to have proposed any measures that would affect people who can pay for all the health care they may need out of their own pockets. Such restrictions would also be impossible to implement, since the rich can always buy medical services abroad. Therefore, blame-based treatment denial will selectively affect only those with limited means. This was noted by Rajendra Persaud long ago in a discussion on whether smokers should be offered bypass surgery: "as wealthy smokers will always be able to afford bypass surgery: the issue is really one of the rights of *poor* smokers to healthcare."[146] Contrary to how it is commonly described, blame-based treatment denial (with or without the ideological embellishment of "luck egalitarianism") will not withdraw health care from people deemed to have caused their own diseases. It will only withdraw health care from *poor* people alleged to have caused their own diseases. This goes against the basic health care principle, expressed already in the Hippocratic oath, of treating those who need it, rather than just those who can pay for it.

8 Conclusion

The following four guidelines can be inferred from our analysis in the previous chapters.

1. In issues of health, distinguish carefully between blame and task responsibility, and give priority to the latter. Industrial safety work became successful when it stopped putting blame responsibility on accident victims and started assigning task responsibilities to employers for creating safer workplaces. Other areas of safety work have learned from this. Patient safety is now based on the insight that we all make mistakes, and much emphasis is put on creating safer equipment and routines that reduce both the probabilities and the consequences of mistakes. As we saw in the previous chapter, in clinical work it is usually counterproductive to blame the patient for having contributed to her own disease. In contrast, assigning realistic task responsibilities to patients can often be helpful.

2. Avoid the single-cause fallacy, and focus on causal factors that can be influenced. Diseases usually have a complex causality involving many causal factors. Focusing on only one of these and calling it "the cause" can be severely misleading. For instance, the tobacco industry has often described individual smokers' decisions to smoke as the cause of smoking. By putting all the blame responsibility on individual smokers, they try to avert our attention from the large effects of their own marketing campaigns. Public health experts, on the contrary, do not look for "the cause" of smoking but instead try to identify causal factors that can be removed or reduced – and this typically includes the industry's marketing campaigns.

3. Distinguish between health-promoting measures on the individual level and the population level. These measures are usually not the same. A person who wants to quit smoking can have use for nicotine patches and inhalers, as well as smoking cessation support individually or in a group. But if our goal is to reduce smoking in the whole population, then we also need to consider measures that make tobacco products less attractive, less accessible, and less affordable. Some examples are age restrictions for the sale of tobacco products, taxes on tobacco products, warning labels, smoke-free public places, and bans on pro-tobacco advertising, promotion, and sponsorship. (See also the discussion on obesity in Section 3.3.)

4. Recognize affordable health care for all as a human right that must be realized in all countries on the globe. As we saw in Section 5.4, universal health care will not be very expensive. Most countries can achieve universal health care with their own resources, if they have not already done so. Low-income countries need some economic assistance. Rich countries have two strong reasons to take joint responsibility for providing that assistance: One reason is the ethical requirement to relieve suffering. The other reason is the simple fact that protection against new epidemics has to be global in order to be efficient. We all need a globally functioning health care infrastructure, strong enough to discover and contain new infectious diseases wherever they make their first appearance.

Notes

1. A distinction can be made between actual and potential blame responsibility, depending on whether or not an event of the type making the person blameworthy has actually occurred. In order not to overload the text with specifications, this distinction will not be made explicitly in what follows.
2. Goodin 1987, 167–168.
3. Hart 1968, 212.
4. Dworkin 1981, 21.
5. Hart 1968, 225.
6. Cane 2002, 31; Duff 1998; van de Poel 2011.
7. Goodin 1987, 167.
8. For a health care example, see Section 7.1.
9. Swuste et al. 2010.
10. Hansson 2022.
11. Verweij & Dawson 2019, 100.
12. Bernstein 2017; Moore 1999, 10.
13. Bernstein 2017; Moore 2009.
14. Kuhn 1971.
15. Berger 1998; Dent 2003.
16. Rizzi & Pedersen 1992.
17. Mill 1843, 327–334.
18. This should not be taken as a reason to embrace a relativistic view of science. On the level of (multiple) causal factors, the arbitrariness involved in selecting "the cause" of an effect does not arise.
19. Agyemang et al. 2015; Ahirwar & Mondal 2019.
20. Afshin et al. 2017; WHO 2021.
21. Adams 2005.
22. Watt 2007.
23. Dicker et al. 2017.
24. Preston 2007; WHO 2019.
25. Naghavi et al. 2017.
26. Brownell et al. 2010.
27. Putnam et al. 2002; Swinburn et al. 2009; Swinburn 2011. The historically dominant role of increased food intake is no reason to neglect the potential role of exercise. In high-income countries, there is currently a trend toward less physical activity and a more sedentary way of life. This is sure to contribute to obesity and bad health. See Guthold et al. 2018; Ng & Popkin 2012.
28. Askari et al. 2020; Monteiro et al. 2018; Robinson el al. 2013. There is also some evidence that frequent consumption of food that is high in both fat and refined sugar can have addictive effects, thus leading to chronic overeating and obesity. However, the concept of food addiction is controversial, and

some researchers consider it to be misleading. See Carter et al. 2016; Hebebrand & Gearhardt 2021.

29. Woodward-Lopez et al. 2010.
30. Goryakin et al. 2017.
31. By mutual agreement, risk exposure can be accepted. See Hansson 2013.
32. Langlands 2011.
33. Cottine 2016; Chrystostomus 1836, 788.
34. Barclift 1991, 14.
35. Lehmann & Ahn 2018.
36. Christakis & Fowler 2007.
37. Christakis & Fowler 2013.
38. Aral & Nicolaides 2017; Christakis & Fowler 2008.
39. Liang et al. 2018; Liang & Zhang 2019.
40. Zaidel 1992, 585.
41. Connolly & Åberg 1993; Edwards et al. 2014.
42. McGhie et al. 2012.
43. Johannessen 1984; Rosenberg & Levenstein 2010.
44. Bachynski 2012, 2216.
45. Hansson 2010.
46. Marteau et al. 2012; Robinson et al. 2013.
47. Gardner et al. 2011; Gardner 2012.
48. "Se eu me contaminei, tá certo? Olha, isso é responsabilidade minha, ninguém tem nada a ver com isso." From an interview on March 16, 2020. Last accessed April 14, 2020, on www.youtube.com/watch?v=M0za 8MSoO64&feature=youtu.be. At 6:58–7:02.
49. Jamrozik et al. 2016.
50. Dixon et al. 2021; Hayman 2019.
51. This was observed by Derek Parfit in his list of "mistakes of moral mathematics": "Even if an act harms no one, this act may be wrong because it is one of a *set* of acts that *together* harm other people" (Parfit 1984, 70). See also Hansson 1999, 2010; Kernohan 2000; Spiekermann 2014; and Nefsky 2017.
52. Smith 2007, 253.
53. Jayes 2016; Lv 2015.
54. Farmer 2017.
55. Mill 1859.
56. Ichikawa et al. 2002.
57. Mill 1865, 340.
58. Mill 1868, 328.
59. Doll 1998.
60. Mill 1870, 385.
61. WHO 2010, 5.
62. Xu et al. 2007.
63. Himmelstein et al. 2019.
64. Crowley et al. 2020.
65. United Nations 1948.

66. United Nations 1976.
67. United Nations 2015.
68. www.who.int/health-topics/universal-health-coverage#tab=tab_1.
69. Garrioch 2011; Thompson 1968, 418–423.
70. Busse et al. 2017.
71. Baines 2013; Digby 2006.
72. Bump 2015.
73. Darker et al. 2018.
74. www.cdc.gov/nchs/fastats/health-insurance.htm. Accessed December 17, 2021.
75. Vaughn 2020, 744.
76. Sen 2015.
77. Sen 2015.
78. Walzer 1983, 91.
79. Chemouni 2018.
80. Chemouni 2018, 92.
81. Emery 2013.
82. WHO, Global health observatory, https://apps.who.int/gho/data/node.main.688.
83. Lu et al. 2017; WHO, Global health observatory, https://apps.who.int/gho/data/node.main.525?lang=en.
84. Harris & Selway 2020; Myers 2017; Nonkhuntod & Yu 2018; Sen 2015.
85. WHO, Global health observatory, https://apps.who.int/gho/data/node.main.525?lang=en.
86. WHO, Global health observatory, https://apps.who.int/gho/data/node.main.688.
87. Bell & Nuzzo 2021.
88. Lagomarsino et al. 2012; Reich et al. 2016.
89. Carcelen et al. 2021.
90. Boozary et al. 2014; Obi 2014.
91. Stenberg et al. 2017; WHO 2017, 12.
92. www.oecd.org/development/financing-sustainable-development/development-finance-standards/official-development-assistance.htm, www.alliedmarketresearch.com/cosmetics-market and https://sipri.org/sites/default/files/Data%20for%20world%20regions%20from%201988%E2%80%932020%20%28pdf%29.pdf. All accessed December 18, 2021.
93. Das et al. 2018.
94. Bruckner 2019.
95. Rhodes 2007.
96. Askitopoulou & Vgontzas 2018; Jouanna 1999, 112–131.
97. Anon. 2005; Litton 2013.
98. American Medical Association 2019.
99. Beisecker & Beisecker 1993.
100. Parsons & Fox 1952.
101. Faden & Beauchamp 1986, 86–100.
102. Beauchamp & Childress 2019.

103. Laine & Davidoff 1996, 155. Cf. Da Rocha 2009, 60–61.
104. Collier 2009.
105. Dietl 1849; Kucharz 1981.
106. Hansson 2015.
107. Loren et al. 2013.
108. Irwig & Bennets 1997.
109. Galmor et al. 2021; Meijers-Heijboer et al. 2001.
110. Ödegård 2007.
111. Rall et al. 2001.
112. Dixon-Woods et al. 2019.
113. Leape & Berwick 2005.
114. Das 2018.
115. Shah et al. 2011.
116. Downey et al. 2010; Ernst 2002; Jagtenberg et al. 2006; Singh & Ernst 2008.
117. This section is based on research performed by the author within the Horizon 2020 research program ETAPAS (Grant agreement number 101004594).
118. Bulten et al. 2020.
119. Grote & Berens 2020; Sand et al. 2021.
120. Tigard 2022.
121. Nyholm 2018, 1209–1210.
122. Kroes & Verbeek 2014.
123. Imming et al. 2006, 824.
124. Waller 2005, 180.
125. For a more detailed discussion of the dissociation between ascriptions of blame and task responsibility to patients, see Hansson 2018. Many other authors have indicated that patients should be entrusted with task responsibilities but not unnecessarily burdened with blame responsibility. See Dougherty 1993, 118; Feiring 2008; Kelley 2005; Pickard 2017; Waller 2005.
126. Brewis et al. 2018; Puhl et al. 2007; Puhl et al. 2020.
127. Keyes et al. 2010.
128. Browne et al. 2013; Else-Quest et al. 2009; Halding et al. 2011.
129. Phelan et al. 2013.
130. Holford et al. 2014.
131. Glannon 1998; Underwood & Baile 1993.
132. Platell 2009. Cf. Lund et al. 2011.
133. Fierlbeck 1996; Persson 2013, 434–435.
134. Major proponents of "luck egalitarianism" include Richard Arneson (2000), G. A. Cohen (1989), Eric Rakowksi (1991), and Shlomi Segall (2010).
135. Dworkin 1981, 293.
136. Cohen 1989, 914. Cf. Guttman & Ressler 2001, 119.
137. Cohen 1989, 922.
138. Sasco et al. 2004.

139. Carbone et al. 2019, 329.
140. Rothschild 2019.
141. Harris 1996, 150.
142. Clavien & Hurst 2020, 188.
143. Ho 2008, 81.
144. Akpan 2014; Rainisch et al. 2015.
145. Clavien & Hurst 2020, 189.
146. Persaud 1995, 284. Cf. Huzum 2009, 206–207.

References

Adams, R. Fast food, obesity, and tort reform: An examination of industry responsibility for public health. *Business and Society Review* 110 (2005): 297–320.

Afshin, A. et al. Health effects of overweight and obesity in 195 countries over 25 years. *New England Journal of Medicine* 377 (2017): 13–27.

Agyemang, S. et al. Obesity in sub-Saharan Africa. In R. S. Ahima, ed., *Metabolic Syndrome. A Comprehensive Textbook*. Cham: Springer, 2015: 41–53.

Ahirwar, R. and Mondal, P. R. Prevalence of obesity in India: A systematic review. *Diabetes & Metabolic Syndrome: Clinical Research & Reviews* 13 (2019): 318–321.

Akpan, N. Ebola Evacuees: Who Are They, Where'd They Go, How'd They Fare? *National Public Radio,* October 15, 2014. www.npr.org/sections/goat sandsoda/2014/10/15/353268622/ebola-evacuees-who-are-they-whered-they-go-howd-they-fare?t=1641937080648. Accessed January 11, 2022.

American Medical Association. *Code of Medical Ethics Opinion 9.7.3*, 2019. www .ama-assn.org/delivering-care/ethics/capital-punishment. Accessed December 31, 2021.

Anonymous. Medical collusion in the death penalty: An American atrocity. *Lancet* 365 (2005): 1361.

Aral, S., and Nicolaides, C. Exercise contagion in a global social network. *Nature Communications* 8 (2017): 1–8.

Arneson, R. J. Luck egalitarianism and prioritarianism. *Ethics* 110 (2000): 339–349.

Askari, M. et al. Ultra-processed food and the risk of overweight and obesity: A systematic review and meta-analysis of observational studies. *International Journal of Obesity* 4 (2020): 2080–2091.

Askitopoulou, H., and Vgontzas, A. N. The relevance of the Hippocratic oath to the ethical and moral values of contemporary medicine. Part II: Interpretation of the Hippocratic oath – today's perspective. *European Spine Journal* 27 (2018): 1491–1500.

Bachynski, K. E. Playing hockey, riding motorcycles, and the ethics of protection. *American Journal of Public Health* 102 (2012): 2214–2220.

Baines, D. From the NIS to the NHS via the floating sixpence. *Prescriber* 24 (2013): 47–49.

Barclift, P. L. In controversy with Saint Augustin: Julian of Eclanum on the nature of sin. *Recherches de Théologie Ancienne et Médiévale* 58 (1991): 5–20.

Beauchamp, T. L., and Childress, J. F. *Principles of Biomedical Ethics*, 8th ed. New York: Oxford University Press, 2019.

Beisecker, A. E., and Beisecker, T. D. Using metaphors to characterize doctor–patient relationships: Paternalism versus consumerism. *Health Communication* 5 (1993): 41–58.

Bell, J. A., and Nuzzo, J. B. *Global Health Security Index: Advancing Collective Action and Accountability amid Global Crisis*, 2021. www.ghsindex.org/wp-content/uploads/2021/12/2021_GHSindexFullReport_Final.pdf.

Berger, R. Understanding science: Why causes are not enough. *Philosophy of Science* 65 (1998): 306–332.

Bernstein, S. Causal proportions and moral responsibility. In D. Shoemaker, ed., *Oxford Studies in Agency and Responsibility*, Volume 4. Oxford: Oxford University Press, 2017: 165–182.

Boozary, A. S., Farmer, P. E., and Jha, A. K. The Ebola outbreak, fragile health systems, and quality as a cure. *JAMA* 312 (2014): 1859–1860.

Brewis, A., SturtzSreetharan, C., and Wutich, A. Obesity stigma as a globalizing health challenge. *Globalization and Health* 14 (2018): 1–6.

Browne, J. L. et al. "I call it the blame and shame disease": A qualitative study about perceptions of social stigma surrounding type 2 diabetes. *BMJ Open* 3 (2013): e003384.

Brownell, K. D. et al. Personal responsibility and obesity: A constructive approach to a controversial issue. *Health Affairs* 29 (2010): 379–387.

Bruckner, T. *The Ignored Pandemic: How Corruption in Healthcare Service Delivery Threatens Universal Health Coverage*. Berlin: Transparency International, 2019.

Bulten et al. Automated deep-learning system for Gleason grading of prostate cancer using biopsies: A diagnostic study. *Lancet Oncology* 21 (2020): 233–241.

Bump, J. B. The long road to universal health coverage: Historical analysis of early decisions in Germany, the United Kingdom, and the United States. *Health Systems & Reform* 1 (2015): 28–38.

Busse, R. et al. Statutory health insurance in Germany: A health system shaped by 135 years of solidarity, self-governance, and competition. *Lancet* 390 (2017): 882–897.

Cane, P. *Responsibility in Law and Morality*. Oxford: Hart Publishing, 2002.

Carbone, S. et al. Obesity, risk of diabetes and role of physical activity, exercise training and cardiorespiratory fitness. *Progress in Cardiovascular Diseases* 62 (2019): 327–333.

Carcelen, A. C. et al. COVID-19 vaccine hesitancy in Zambia: A glimpse at the possible challenges ahead for COVID-19 vaccination rollout in sub-Saharan Africa. *Human Vaccines & Immunotherapeutics*, 2021. Published online, DOI: 10.1080/21645515.2021.1948784.

Carter, A. et al. The neurobiology of "food addiction" and its implications for obesity treatment and policy. *Annual Review of Nutrition* 36 (2016): 105–128.

Chemouni, B. The political path to universal health coverage: Power, ideas and community-based health insurance in Rwanda. *World Development* 106 (2018): 87–98.

Christakis, N. A., and Fowler, J. H. The spread of obesity in a large social network over 32 years. *New England Journal of Medicine* 357 (2007): 370–379.

Christakis, N. A., and Fowler, J. H. The collective dynamics of smoking in a large social network. *New England Journal of Medicine* 358 (2008): 2249–2258.

Christakis, N. A., and Fowler, J. H. Social contagion theory: examining dynamic social networks and human behavior. *Statistics in Medicine* 32 (2013): 556–577.

Chrystostomus, J. *Diatriba ad opus imperfectum in Matthaeum*. In J. Chrystostomus, *Opera Omnia*, Tomus Sextus. Paris: Gaume Fratres, 1836: 731–972.

Clavien, C., and Hurst, S. The undeserving sick? An evaluation of patients' responsibility for their health condition. *Cambridge Quarterly of Healthcare Ethics* 29 (2020): 175–191.

Cohen, G. A. On the currency of egalitarian justice. *Ethics* 99 (1989): 906–944.

Collier, R. Legumes, lemons and streptomycin: A short history of the clinical trial. *Canadian Medical Association Journal* 180 (2009): 23–24.

Connolly, T., and Åberg, L. Some contagion models of speeding. *Accident Analysis & Prevention* 25 (1993): 57-66.

Cottine, C. Role modeling in an early Confucian context. *Journal of Value Inquiry* 50 (2016): 797–819.

Crowley, R. et al. Envisioning a better US health care system for all: coverage and cost of care. *Annals of Internal Medicine* 172 (2020): S7–S32.

Da Rocha, A. C. Back to basics in bioethics: Reconciling patient autonomy with physician responsibility. *Philosophy Compass* 4 (2009): 56–68.

Darker, C. D., Donnelly-Swift, E., and Whiston, L. Demographic factors and attitudes that influence the support of the general public for the introduction of universal healthcare in Ireland: A national survey. *Health Policy* 122 (2018): 147–156.

Das, J. et al. Rethinking assumptions about delivery of healthcare: Implications for universal health coverage. *BMJ* 361 (2018): k1716.

Dent, E. B. The interaction model: An alternative to the direct cause and effect construct for mutually causal organizational phenomena. *Foundations of Science* 8 (2003): 295–314.

Dicker, D. et al. Global, regional, and national age-sex-specific mortality and life expectancy, 1950–2017: A systematic analysis for the Global Burden of Disease Study 2017. *Lancet* 392 (2017): 1684–1735.

Dietl, J. *Der Aderlass in der Lungenentzündung.* Wien: Kaulfuss Witwe, Prandel & Comp., 1849.

Digby, A. The economic and medical significance of the British National Health Insurance Act, 1911. In M. Gorsky and S. Sheard, eds., *Financing Medicine. The British Experience since 1750.* Abingdon: Routledge, 2006: 182–198.

Dixon, M. G. et al. Progress toward regional measles elimination – worldwide, 2000–2020. *Morbidity and Mortality Weekly Report* 70 (2021): 1563–1569.

Dixon-Woods, M. et al. Improving employee voice about transgressive or disruptive behavior: A case study. *Academic Medicine* 94 (2019): 579–585.

Doll, R. Uncovering the effects of smoking: Historical perspective. *Statistical Methods in Medical Research* 7 (1998): 87–117.

Dougherty, C. J. Bad faith and victim-blaming: The limits of health promotion. *Health Care Analysis* 1 (1993): 111–119.

Downey, L. et al. Pediatric vaccination and vaccine-preventable disease acquisition: Associations with care by complementary and alternative medicine providers. *Maternal and Child Health Journal* 14 (2010): 922–930.

Duff, R. A. Responsibility. *Routledge Encyclopedia of Philosophy.* Taylor and Francis, 1998. www.rep.routledge.com/articles/thematic/responsibility/v-1.

Dworkin, G. Voluntary health risks and public policy: Taking risks, assessing responsibility. *Hastings Centre Report* 11 (1981): 26–31.

Dworkin, R. What is equality? Part 2: Equality of resources. *Philosophy and Public Affairs* 10 (1981): 283–345.

Edwards, J. et al. A framework for conceptualising traffic safety culture. *Transportation Research Part F* 26 (2014): 293–302.

Else-Quest, N. M. et al. Perceived stigma, self-blame, and adjustment among lung, breast and prostate cancer patients. *Psychology and Health* 24 (2009): 949–964.

Emery, N. Rwanda's historic health recovery: What the U.S. might learn. *The Atlantic*, February 20, 2013.

Ernst, E. A systematic review of systematic reviews of homeopathy. *British Journal of Clinical Pharmacology* 54 (2002): 577–582.

Faden, R. R., and Beauchamp, T. *A History and Theory of Informed Consent.* New York: Oxford University Press, 1986.

Farmer, C. M. Relationship of traffic fatality rates to maximum state speed limits. *Traffic Injury Prevention* 18 (2017): 375–380.

Feiring, E. Lifestyle, responsibility and justice. *Journal of Medical Ethics* 34 (2008): 33–36.

Fierlbeck, K. Policy and ideology: The politics of post-reform health policy in the United Kingdom. *International Journal of Health Services* 26 (1996): 529–546.

Galmor, L. et al. Time trends in uptake rates of risk-reducing mastectomy in Israeli asymptomatic BRCA1 and BRCA2 mutation carriers. *Breast Cancer Research and Treatment* 185 (2021): 391–399.

Gardner, B. Habit as automaticity, not frequency. *European Health Psychologist* 14 (2012): 32–36.

Gardner, B., de Bruijn, G.-J., and Lally, P. A systematic review and meta-analysis of applications of the self-report habit index to nutrition and physical activity behaviours. *Annals of Behavioral Medicine* 42 (2011): 174–187.

Garrioch, D. Mutual aid societies in eighteenth-century Paris. *French History & Civilization* 4 (2011): 22–33.

Glannon, W. Responsibility, alcoholism and liver transplantation. *Journal of Medicine and Philosophy* 23 (1998): 31–49.

Goodin, R. E. Apportioning responsibilities. *Law and Philosophy* 6 (1987): 167–185.

Goryakin, Y., Monsivais, P., and Suhrcke, M. Soft drink prices, sales, body mass index and diabetes: Evidence from a panel of low-, middle- and high-income countries. *Food Policy* 73 (2017): 88–94.

Grote, T., and Berens, P. On the ethics of algorithmic decision-making in healthcare. *Journal of Medical Ethics* 46 (2020): 205–211.

Guthold, R. et al. Worldwide trends in insufficient physical activity from 2001 to 2016: A pooled analysis of 358 population-based surveys with 1.9 million participants. *Lancet Global Health* 6 (2018): e1077-e1086.

Guttman, N., and Ressler, W. H. On being responsible: Ethical issues in appeals to personal responsibility in health campaigns. *Journal of Health Communication: International Perspectives* 6 (2001): 117–136.

Halding, A.-G., Heggdal, K., and Wahl, A. Experiences of self-blame and stigmatisation for self-infliction among individuals living with COPD. *Scandinavian Journal of Caring Sciences* 25 (2011): 100–107.

Hansson, S. O. The moral significance of indetectable effects. *Risk* 10 (1999): 101–108.

Hansson, S. O. The harmful influence of decision theory on ethics. *Ethical Theory and Moral Practice* 13 (2010): 585–593.

Hansson, S. O. *The Ethics of Risk. Ethical Analysis in an Uncertain World.* New York: Palgrave Macmillan, 2013.

Hansson, S. O. Experiments before science. What science learned from technological experiments. In S. O. Hansson, ed., *The Role of Technology in Science. Philosophical Perspectives.* Dordrecht: Springer, 2015: 81–110.

Hansson, S. O. The ethics of making patients responsible. *Cambridge Quarterly of Healthcare Ethics* 27 (2018): 87–92.

Hansson, S. O. Responsibility in road traffic. In K. Edvardsson Björnberg, S. O. Hansson, M.-Å. Belin, and C. Tingvall, eds., *The Vision Zero Handbook.* Cham: Springer, 2022.

Harris, J. Could we hold people responsible for their own adverse health? *Journal of Contemporary Health Law & Policy* 12 (1996): 147–153.

Harris, J., and Selway, J. Exchange: Explaining the passage of universal healthcare in Thailand. *Journal of East Asian Studies* 20 (2020): 99–119.

Hart, H. L. A. *Punishment and Responsibility. Essays in the Philosophy of Law.* Oxford: Oxford University Press, 1968.

Hayman, D. T. S. Measles vaccination in an increasingly immunized and developed world. *Human Vaccines & Immunotherapeutics* 15 (2019): 28–33.

Hebebrand, J., and Gearhardt, A. N. The concept of "food addiction" helps inform the understanding of overeating and obesity: NO. *American Journal of Clinical Nutrition* 113 (2021): 268–273.

Himmelstein, D. U. et al. Medical bankruptcy: Still common despite the Affordable Care Act. *American Journal of Public Health* 109 (2019): 431–433.

Ho, D. When good organs go to bad people. *Bioethics* 22 (2008): 77–83.

Holford, T. R. et al. Tobacco control and the reduction in smoking-related premature deaths in the United States, 1964–2012. *JAMA* 311 (2014): 164–171.

Huzum, E. The principle of responsibility for illness and its application in the allocation of health care. A critical analysis. In B. Olaru (ed.), *Autonomy, Responsibility, and Health Care, Critical Reflections.* Bucharest: Zeta Books, 2009: 191–218.

Ichikawa, M., Nakahara, S., and Wakai, S. Mortality of front-seat occupants attributable to unbelted rear-seat passengers in car crashes. *Lancet* 359 (2002): 43–44.

Imming, P., Sinning, C., and Meyer, A. Drugs, their targets and the nature and number of drug targets. *Nature Reviews Drug Discovery* 5 (2006): 821–834.

Irwig, L., and Bennetts, A. Quality of life after breast conservation or mastectomy: A systematic review. *Australian and New Zealand Journal of Surgery* 67 (1997): 750–754.

Jagtenberg, T. et al. Evidence-based medicine and naturopathy. *Journal of Alternative & Complementary Medicine* 12 (2006): 323–328.

Jamrozik, E., Handfield, T. and Selgelid, M. J. Victims, vectors and villains: Are those who opt out of vaccination morally responsible for the deaths of others? *Journal of Medical Ethics* 42 (2016): 762–768.

Jayes, L. et al. SmokeHaz: Systematic reviews and meta-analyses of the effects of smoking on respiratory health. *Chest* 150 (2016): 164–179.

Johannessen, G. *Historical Perspective on Seat Belt Restraint Systems*. SAE Technical Paper no. 840392. Society of Automotive Engineers, 1984.

Jouanna, J. *Hippocrates*. Baltimore: Johns Hopkins University Press, 1999.

Kelley, M. Limits on patient responsibility. *Journal of Medicine and Philosophy* 30 (2005): 189–206.

Kernohan, A. Individual acts and accumulative consequences. *Philosophical Studies* 97 (2000): 343–366.

Keyes, K. M. et al. Stigma and treatment for alcohol disorders in the United States. *American Journal of Epidemiology* 172 (2010): 1364–1372.

Kroes, P., and Verbeek, P.-P., eds. *The Moral Status of Technical Artefacts*. Springer: Dordrecht, 2014.

Kucharz, E. The life and achievements of Joseph Dietl. *Clio Medica. Acta Academiae Internationalis Historiae Medicinae Amsterdam* 16 (1981): 25–35.

Kuhn, T. S. La notion de causalité dans le devéloppement de la physique. In M. Bunge (ed.), *Les Théories de la Causalité*. Paris: Presses univ. de France, 1971: 4–15.

Lagomarsino, G. et al. Moving towards universal health coverage: Health insurance reforms in nine developing countries in Africa and Asia. *Lancet* 380 (2012): 933–943.

Laine, C., and Davidoff, F. Patient-centered medicine: A professional evolution. *JAMA* 275 (1996): 152–156.

Langlands, R. Roman exempla and situation ethics: Valerius Maximus and Cicero de Officiis. *Journal of Roman Studies* 101 (2011): 100–122.

Leape, L. L., and Berwick, D. M. Five years after To Err Is Human: What have we learned? *JAMA* 293 (2005): 2384–2390.

Lehmann, S., and Ahn, Y.-Y. *Complex Spreading Phenomena in Social Systems. Influence and Contagion in Real-World Social Networks*. Cham: Springer, 2018.

Liang, H., and Zhang, S. Impact of supervisors' safety violations on an individual worker within a construction crew. *Safety Science* 120 (2019): 679–691.

Liang, H. et al. The impact of coworkers' safety violations on an individual worker: A social contagion effect within the construction crew. *International Journal of Environmental Research and Public Health* 15 (2018): 773.

Litton, P. J. Physician participation in executions, the morality of capital punishment, and the practical implications of their relationship. *Journal of Law, Medicine and Ethics* 41 (2013): 333–352.

Loren, A. W. et al. Fertility preservation for patients with cancer: American Society of Clinical Oncology clinical practice guideline update. *Journal of Clinical Oncology* 31 (2013): 2500–2510.

Lu, C., Cook, B., and Desmond, C. Does foreign aid crowd out government investments? Evidence from rural health centres in Rwanda. *BMJ Global Health* 2 (2017): e000364.

Lund, T. B., Sandøe, P., and Lassen, J. Attitudes to publicly funded obesity treatment and prevention. *Obesity* 19 (2011): 1580–1585.

Lv, X. et al. Risk of all-cause mortality and cardiovascular disease associated with secondhand smoke exposure: A systematic review and meta-analysis. *International Journal of Cardiology* 199 (2015): 106–115.

Marteau, T. M., Hollands, G. J., and Fletcher, P. C. Changing human behavior to prevent disease: The importance of targeting automatic processes. *Science* 337 (2012): 1492–1495.

McGhie, A., Lewis, I., and Hyde, M. K. The influence of conformity and group identity on drink walking intentions: Comparing intentions to drink walk across risky pedestrian crossing scenarios. *Accident Analysis and Prevention* 45 (2012): 639–645.

Meijers-Heijboer, H. et al. Breast cancer after prophylactic bilateral mastectomy in women with a BRCA1 or BRCA2 mutation. *New England Journal of Medicine* 345 (2001): 159–164.

Mill, J. S. *A System of Logic*. In J. S. Mill, *Collected Works of John Stuart Mill*, volume 7. Toronto: University of Toronto Press, 1843/1996.

Mill, J. S. *On Liberty*. In J. S. Mill, *Collected Works of John Stuart Mill*, volume 18. Toronto: University of Toronto Press, 1859/1977: 213–310.

Mill, J. S. *Auguste Comte and Positivism*. In J. S. Mill, *Collected Works of John Stuart Mill*, volume 10. Toronto: University of Toronto Press, 1865/1969: 261–368.

Mill, J. S. *Smoking in Railway Carriages*. In J. S. Mill, *Collected Works of John Stuart Mill*, volume 28. Toronto: University of Toronto Press, 1868/1988: 328.

Mill, J. S. *The Education Bill*. In J. S. Mill, *Collected Works of John Stuart Mill*, volume 29. Toronto: University of Toronto Press, 1870/1988: 381–386.

Monteiro, C. A. et al. The UN decade of nutrition, the NOVA food classification and the trouble with ultra-processing. *Public Health Nutrition* 21 (2018): 5–17.

Moore, M. S. Causation and responsibility. *Social Philosophy and Policy* 16 (1999): 1–51.

Moore, M. S. *Causation and Responsibility: An Essay in Law, Morals, and Metaphysics*. New York: Oxford University Press, 2009.

Myers, D. US healthcare: A "disaster" of a system. *Pitt Political Review* 12 (2017): 16–19.

Naghavi, M. et al. Global, regional, and national age-sex specific mortality for 264 causes of death, 1980–2016: A systematic analysis for the Global Burden of Disease Study 2016. *Lancet* 390 (2017): 1151–1210.

Nefsky, J. Collective harm and the inefficacy problem. *Philosophy Compass* 14 (2019): e12587.

Ng, S. W., and Popkin, B. M. Time use and physical activity: A shift away from movement across the globe. *Obesity Reviews* 13 (2012): 659–680.

Nonkhuntod, R., and Yu, S. Lessons from Thailand: Universal healthcare achievements and challenges. *International Journal of Social Economics* 45 (2018): 387–401.

Nyholm, S. Attributing agency to automated systems: Reflections on human–robot collaborations and responsibility-loci. *Science and Engineering Ethics* 24 (2018): 1201–1219.

Obi, E. C. Ebola virus disease: A case for shared national and global responsibility in a global health crisis. *Ethics in Biology, Engineering and Medicine: An International Journal* 5 (2014): 139–147.

Ödegård, S. Tre uppmärksammade rättsfall i svensk hälso- och sjukvård. In S. Ödegård, ed., *I rättvisans namn: ansvar, skuld och säkerhet i vården*. Stockholm: Liber, 2007: 11–60.

Parfit, D. *Reasons and Persons*. Oxford: Clarendon Press, 1984.

Parsons, T., and Fox, R. Illness, therapy, and the modern urban American family. *Journal of Social Issues* 8 (1952): 31–44.

Persaud, R. Smoker's rights to health care. *Journal of Medical Ethics* 21 (1995): 281–287.

Persson, K. The right perspective on responsibility for ill health. *Medicine, Health Care and Philosophy* 16 (2013): 429–441.

Phelan S. M. et al. Stigma, perceived blame, self-blame, and depressive symptoms in men with colorectal cancer. *Psycho-Oncology* 22 (2013): 65–73.

Pickard, H. Responsibility without blame for addiction. *Neuroethics* 10 (2017): 169–180.

Platell, A. Sorry, why should the NHS treat people for being fat? *Daily Mail* online, February 27, 2009. www.dailymail.co.uk/debate/article-1156678/AMANDA-PLATELL-Sorry-NHS-treat-people-fat.html-. Accessed December 25, 2021.

Preston, S. H. The changing relation between mortality and level of economic development. *International Journal of Epidemiology* 36 (2007): 484–490.

Puhl, R. M., Himmelstein, M. S., and Pearl, R. L. Weight stigma as a psychosocial contributor to obesity. *American Psychologist* 75 (2020): 274–289.

Puhl, R. M., Moss-Racusin, C. A., and Schwartz, M. B. Internalization of weight bias: Implications for binge eating and emotional well-being. *Obesity* 15 (2007): 19–23.

Putnam, J., Allshouse, J., and Kantor, L. US per capita food supply trends: More calories, refined carbohydrates, and fats. *Food Review* 25 (2002): 2–15.

Rainisch, G. et al. Estimating Ebola treatment needs, United States. *Emerging Infectious Diseases* 21 (2015): 1273–1275.

Rakowski, E. *Equal Justice*. New York: Oxford University Press, 1991.

Rall, M. et al. Patient safety and errors in medicine: Development, prevention and analyses of incidents. *Anasthesiologie Intensivmedizin Notfallmedizin Schmerztherapie* 36 (2001): 321–330.

Reich, M. R. et al. Moving towards universal health coverage: Lessons from 11 country studies. *Lancet* 387 (2016): 811–816.

Rhodes, R. The professional responsibilities of medicine. In R. Rhodes, L. P. Francis, and A. Silvers (eds.), *The Blackwell Guide to Medical Ethics*. Malden, MA: Blackwell, 2007: 71–87.

Rizzi, D. A., and Pedersen, S. A. Causality in medicine: Towards a theory and terminology. *Theoretical Medicine* 13 (1992): 233–254.

Robinson, E. et al. Eating attentively: A systematic review and meta-analysis of the effect of food intake memory and awareness on eating. *American Journal of Clinical Nutrition* 97 (2013): 728–742.

Rosenberg, B., and Levenstein, C. Social factors in occupational health: A history of hard hats. *New Solutions: A Journal of Environmental and Occupational Health Policy* 20 (2010): 239–249.

Rothschild, M. Cruel and unusual prison healthcare: A look at the Arizona class action litigation of Parsons v. Ryan and systemic deficiencies of private health services in prison. *Arizona Law Review* 61 (2019): 945–981.

Sand, M., Durán, J. M., and Jongsma, K. R. Responsibility beyond design: Physicians' requirements for ethical medical AI. *Bioethics*, 2021, published online, https://doi.org/10.1111/bioe.12887.

Sasco, A. J., Secretan, M. B., and Straif, K. Tobacco smoking and cancer: A brief review of recent epidemiological evidence. *Lung Cancer* 45 (2004): S3–S9.

Segall, S. *Health, Luck and Justice*. Princeton: Princeton University Press, 2010.

Sen, A. Universal healthcare: The affordable dream. *Guardian,* January 6, 2015.

Shah, N. M., Brieger, W. R., and Peters, D. H. Can interventions improve health services from informal private providers in low- and middle-income countries? A comprehensive review of the literature. *Health Policy and Planning* 26 (2011): 275–287.

Singh, S., and Ernst, E. *Trick or Treatment. Alternative Medicine on Trial.* London: Corgi Books, 2008.

Smith, G. P. Cigarette smoking as a public health hazard: Crafting common law and legislative strategies. *Michigan State University Journal of Medicine & Law* 11 (2007): 251–302.

Spiekermann, K. Small impacts and imperceptible effects: Causing harm with others. *Midwest Studies in Philosophy* 38 (2014): 75–90.

Stenberg, K. et al. Financing transformative health systems towards achievement of the health Sustainable Development Goals: A model for projected resource needs in 67 low-income and middle-income countries. *Lancet Global Health* 5 (2017): e875–e887.

Swinburn, B., Sacks, G., and Ravussin, E. Increased food energy supply is more than sufficient to explain the US epidemic of obesity. *American Journal of Clinical Nutrition* 90 (2009): 1453–1456.

Swinburn B. et al. The global obesity pandemic: Shaped by global drivers and local environments. *Lancet* 378 (2011): 804–814.

Swuste, P., van Gulijk, C., and Zwaard, W. Safety metaphors and theories, a review of the occupational safety literature of the US, UK and The Netherlands, till the first part of the 20th century. *Safety Science* 48 (2010): 1000–1018.

Thompson, E. P. *The Making of the English Working Class*. Harmondsworth: Penguin, 1968.

Tigard, D. W. Big data and the threat to moral responsibility in healthcare. In G. Richter et al. (eds.), *Datenreiche Medizin und das Problem der*

Einwilligung. Ethische, rechtliche und sozialwissenschaftliche Perspektiven. Berlin: Springer, 2022: 11–25.

Underwood, M. J., and Bailey, S. J. Coronary bypass surgery should not be offered to smokers. *BMJ* 306 (1993): 1047–1050.

United Nations. *The Universal Declaration of Human Rights.* www.un.org/en/about-us/universal-declaration-of-human-right, 1948.

United Nations. *International Covenant on Economic, Social and Cultural Rights.* www.ohchr.org/en/professionalinterest/pages/cescr.aspx, 1976.

United Nations. *Transforming Our World: The 2030 Agenda for Sustainable Development.* https://sdgs.un.org/2030agenda, 2015.

van de Poel, I. The relation between forward-looking and backward-looking responsibility. In N. A. Vincent, I. van de Poel, and J. van den Hoven (eds.), *Moral Responsibility.* Dordrecht: Springer, 2011: 37–52.

Vaughn, L. *Bioethics. Principles, Issues, and Cases*, 4th ed. New York: Oxford University Press, 2020.

Verweij, M., and Dawson, A. Sharing responsibility: Responsibility for health is not a zero-sum game. *Public Health Ethics* 12 (2019): 99–102.

Waller, B. N. Responsibility and health. *Cambridge Quarterly of Healthcare Ethics* 14 (2005): 177–188.

Walzer, M. *Spheres of Justice. A Defense of Pluralism and Equality.* New York: Basic Books, 1983.

Watt, R. G. From victim blaming to upstream action: Tackling the social determinants of oral health inequalities. *Community Dentistry and Oral Epidemiology* 35 (2007): 1–11.

WHO. *The World Health Report 2010: Health systems financing. The path to universal coverage.* Geneva: World Health Organization, 2010.

WHO. *Together on the road to universal health coverage.* Geneva: World Health Organization, 2017.

WHO. *WHO global report on trends in prevalence of tobacco use 2000–2025*, 3rd edition. Geneva: World Health Organization, 2019. https://apps.who.int/iris/bitstream/handle/10665/330221/9789240000032-eng.pdf.

WHO. *Obesity and overweight.* Geneva: World Health Organization, 2021. www.who.int/en/news-room/fact-sheets/detail/obesity-and-overweight.

Woodward-Lopez, G., Kao, J., and Ritchie, L. To what extent have sweetened beverages contributed to the obesity epidemic? *Public Health Nutrition* 14 (2010): 499–509.

Xu, K. et al. Protecting households from catastrophic health spending. *Health Affairs* 26 (2007): 972–983.

Zaidel, D. M. A modeling perspective on the culture of driving. *Accident Analysis and Prevention* 24 (1992): 585–597.

Cambridge Elements ≡

Bioethics and Neuroethics

Thomasine Kushner

California Pacific Medical Center, San Francisco

Thomasine Kushner, PhD, is the founding Editor of the *Cambridge Quarterly of Healthcare Ethics* and coordinates the International Bioethics Retreat, where bioethicists share their current research projects, the Cambridge Consortium for Bioethics Education, a growing network of global bioethics educators, and the Cambridge-ICM Neuroethics Network, which provides a setting for leading brain scientists and ethicists to learn from each other.

About the Series

Bioethics and neuroethics play pivotal roles in today's debates in philosophy, science, law, and health policy. With the rapid growth of scientific and technological advances, their importance will only increase. This series provides focused and comprehensive coverage in both disciplines consisting of foundational topics, current subjects under discussion and views toward future developments.

Cambridge Elements ≡

Bioethics and Neuroethics

Printed in the United States
by Baker & Taylor Publisher Services